MW00768148

WHATEVER IS *Lovely*

DESIGN *for* AN ELEGANT SPIRIT

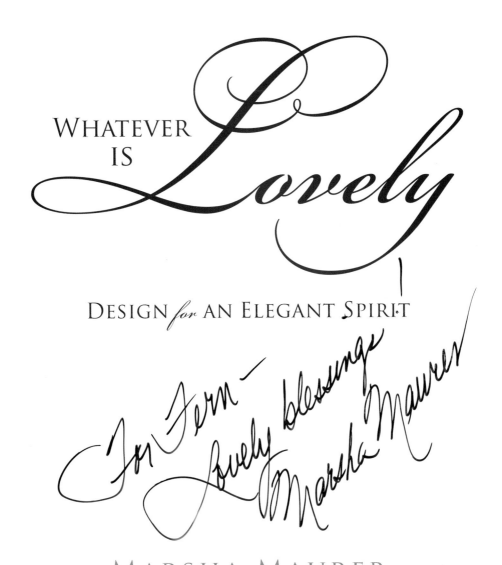

For Fern—
Lovely blessings
Marsha Maurer

MARSHA MAURER

WHATEVER IS *Lovely:*
DESIGN FOR AN ELEGANT SPIRIT

Published by Carpenter's Son Publishing, Franklin, Tennessee

Published in association with Larry Carpenter of Christian Book Services, LLC
www.christianbookservices.com

Edited by: Lorraine Bosse-Smith

Cover and Interior Design: Jade Novak

Photography ©: iii thinkstock/istockphoto; 5 Cathy K; 7 pontuse; 9 Bob Star; 10 Noche; 14 gerbrak; 16 Stefan; 19 geishaboy500; 23 remind; 26 Steven Arnold-Dreamstime.com; 29 Edgaras Kurauskas-Dreamstime.com; 31 Stephen Denness-Dreamstime.com; 34 Vivek Chugh; 35 www.imageafter.com; 38 Susan Fox; 41 Josef F. Stuefer; 42 felinda-Fotolia.com; 43 Adrian van Leen; 45 Olga Tkachenko; 47 Chris Leachman-Dreamstime.com; 49 Linda H.; 50 mimiliz; 51 Michael Flippo-Dreamstime.com; 53 thebittenword.com; 56 losiek; 60 Grauvision-Dreamstime.com; 61 M Connors; 62 Hewac-Fotolia.com; 65 Vroom Broom; 69 Olga Kadroff; 71 Elnur; 72 Jasmin Merdan-Fotolia.com; 73 hotblack; 77 Pavlos Rekas-Dreamstime.com; 79 Ben Fredericson; 81 Anita Patterson; 84 Lia Koltyrina; 85 Mirceax-Dreamstime.com; 88 Cecilia Lim-Dreamstime.com; 90 Scott Robinson; 93 priyanphoenix; 96 Nick Stubbs-Dreamstime.com; 97 Lorna-Dreamstime.com; 98 Alena Brozova; 99 Mirek Hejnicki; 101 www.zabara.org; 104 Sergey Gavrilchev-Dreamstime.com; 105 audreyjm529; 107 Dainis Derics; 110 1000 Words-Dreamstime.com; 112 Piotr Skubisz-Dreamstime.com; 115 Arkady; 117 Serge Villa-Dreamstime.com; 120 Dora Mitsonia; 121 seier; 123 Jostein Hauge; 124 Andrew Shaw-Dreamstime.com; 127 Clearly Ambiguous; 129 brainloc; Berthold Werner; 132 Alexey Koverznev-Fotolia.com; 135 Natalia Lisovskaya-Dreamstime.com; 136 Bagwold-Dreamstime.com; 137 Carlos Caetano; 141 lululemon athletica; 145 Braydawg; 147 b. k.; 148 Birute Vijeikiene-Dreamsland.com; 149 Mark Stout Photography; 152 Dave Morris; 153 silver-john; 154 Mathew Ingram; 155 Eky Studio; 156 bcmom; 158 Nataliya Hora; 163 Galyna Andrushko; 164 Iakov Filimonov-Dreamstime.com; 166 Andreja Donko-Dreamstime.com; 168 Vladimir Voronin; 169 Elnur Amikishiyev; 171 David Biagi; 172 David Schauer; 175 Robyn Mackenzie; 176 Clarita; 178 Pascal Thauvin; 181 Irafael; 184 pontuse; 186 Simona Dumitru.

Printed in China

978-0-9835571-6-6

TABLE OF CONTENTS

*With gratitude to all my sources of inspiration,
especially to my parents and family; to Norma;
and always, to my dear Michael*

"WHATEVER IS TRUE, WHATEVER IS NOBLE,
WHATEVER IS RIGHT, WHATEVER IS PURE,
WHATEVER IS LOVELY, WHATEVER IS ADMIRABLE——
IF ANYTHING IS EXCELLENT OR PRAISEWORTHY——
THINK ABOUT SUCH THINGS."

Paul's Letter to the Philippians 4:8

Introduction

We have all seen her—the elegant woman—refined, gracious, and lovely. Elegance is easy to recognize. We may not be able to describe elegance exactly, but we can easily identify a woman who has it. Elegance is far more than physical bearing; it is a manner of spirit.

In its original form, the word "elegance" means to elect or select. This meaning suggests that elegance can be achieved by any woman. If we are willing to examine our choices, we can cultivate an elegant spirit.

This refinement is not additional work we need to squeeze into an already crowded life; it is simply a matter of immersing ourselves in the qualities and virtues we desire until they become intrinsic. A Biblical verse puts it this way: *"Whatever is true, whatever is noble, whatever is right, whatever is pure, whatever is lovely, whatever is admirable—if anything is excellent or praiseworthy—think about such things"* (Philippians 4:8).

As these lines suggest, what we think about, hear, watch, and read; the people with whom we associate; the ideas we entertain; the activities in which we engage; all that we consume and absorb—these are who we become. And while we may not control all that touches our lives, we do have choices. This book is about those choices.

*E*VEN IF WE FEEL LESS THAN CREATIVE, WE MIGHT SURPRISE OURSELVES WITH OUR DESIGN TALENTS.

Humans are naturally creative beings. Even if we feel less than creative, we might surprise ourselves with our design talents. We plan menus and create meals; we select plants and arrange a garden; we create a business plan and execute it; we choose pieces and fashion a wardrobe; we gather our favorite possessions and decorate a room. Design is not just for artistic endeavors; it is also for creating the women we would like to become.

When we set about to create a room, a garden, a wardrobe, or a dinner party, we rely on principles of design to make those efforts successful and pleasing. We may not consciously consider our decisions, choices, and selections in terms of design, but we likely bring to those creative tasks skills of judgment which we have acquired and developed.

Personally, I learned home design from childhood play with discarded curtains and chairs; from helping my mother in regularly redecorating our girlhood bedroom; from close reading of home magazines and design volumes; from redesigning our military quarters with frequent moves; from visits to museums and historic homes; from attentive forays through antique shops and European flea markets; and from careful acquisitions on a limited budget.

I learned garden design from my mother as she cultivated flowers; from visits to nurseries and professionally designed gardens; from tantalizing garden catalogs, magazines, and books, gaining confidence from my earliest tentative efforts.

I learned wardrobe design by creating costumes of thrift-shop scarves and high-heels, hats, skirts, and feathers from my mother's closet; from her experienced sewing advice about texture, color, hand,

and drape of fabric, fitting, construction, and finishing of garments; from fashion magazines and books about historic style setters; from surviving the worst of the 70s trends; from travels in France; and from training a critical eye on my personal fashion evolution.

I learned how to design and prepare food from European fresh markets; from dining delights of international travel, inspiring me to replicate dishes in our own kitchen; from studying recipes and techniques; from trying new menus on anyone who would share our table; and from entertaining often.

I learned spiritual design by attending church, Sunday school, Christian elementary school and college, guided and inspired by my parents and teachers, applying Biblical tenets to my own spiritual life.

Many women will have similar experiences in acquiring the elements of design, which they apply to living. Those of us who may feel less than competent in making furniture, apparel, landscaping, or entertaining selections, go to experts for professional design assistance. We refine our homes and appearance for the pleasure and satisfaction they contribute to our living.

While we are so attentive and discerning in designing many aspects of our lives, how curious that we often give so little care to designing that which most affects the quality and happiness of our lives, that is, the women we are ourselves. Often we spend more time choosing throw pillows or shoes than considering the personal qualities and virtues we want to nurture.

For most of us, through the years, interests dominate, proprieties dictate, choices narrow, and habits calcify, until we emerge as the women we now see reflected in our morning mirror. I do not mean our physical image—hair color, body shape, and profile, but the inner person we project. We like parts of the women we have become, but we wish we could transform other qualities to more closely resemble the image we would like to project. It is never too late to become that elegant spirit we aspire to be.

We need no innate artistic talent to redesign ourselves, our attitudes, or our behavior; we have lots of sources to inspire us. This compendium of musings, stories, and quotations from throughout history suggest the timeless embrace of universal virtues. The pages ahead apply principles of design to encourage our discriminating selves; to offer alternatives we may not have considered; to inspire fresh ways of seeing, ideas to ponder, thoughts for reflecting, possibilities for becoming. As discriminating women, we select carefully and claim those spiritual values ordained by God. We discern differences among options, seek divine guidance, and make thoughtful judgments about who we want to be, shaping our preferences for whatever is lovely.

Anticipation

Entrances establish our expectations. At the end of our shady, ivy-lined walkway, we replaced overgrown shrubs with a bright spot of flowering color, inviting our guests to turn a corner and climb steps to our front door. We designed the space to create a welcoming approach, hinting at hospitality within. Sometimes I wonder why we bother. Despite my efforts to direct guests to our front entry, they insist on using the back door, convenient from the drive, through a catch-all garage and non-descript laundry room. Clothes basket and cat box are hardly the prelude I want to provide. We have hung an imposing French film poster in the laundry in hopes guests will overlook the arrival when they find a chilled glass in their hand, soft jazz playing, and candles lit. Our early overtures in greeting our guests are designed to induce the spirit of a convivial evening, to inspire anticipation.

Anticipation is the heartbeat of life. Without hope, we cannot survive. Looking forward to satisfying labors and fulfilling relationships engenders joy. While we are rarely eager for every experience a day may hold, a bright sense of expectancy can ease the dull and difficult and enable us to embrace the blessings which unfold.

JOYS OF THIS WORLD INSPIRE EAGER YEARNING FOR ALL THAT LIES AHEAD. My Brazilian friend tells me that in her native country, spike-leaf snake plants often grace the entrance of a home, their points deterring evil spirits. Others say spires of the plant point to heaven—now that is anticipation! God intends for us to live forever in His grace. Joys of this world inspire eager yearning for all that lies ahead. As Nathaniel Hawthorne muses, "Our Creator would never have made such lovely days and have given us the deep hearts to enjoy them, above and beyond all thought, unless we were meant to be immortal."

Balance

B ecause nothing in life or nature is perfectly identical, matched pairs—of lamps, cushions, chairs—strike me as a little too tidy. I use pairs judiciously in groupings. Balance is critical to décor, of course, but I prefer asymmetry to repetition. In my dining room, I have thrown great swaths of drapery over a rod, knotted floor level on one side and mid-window on the other. Balance comes from an étagère stationed near the shorter side. Uniformity feels inflexible to me. Two unmatched chairs of similar scale, echoing a color or pattern, make a more inviting conversational grouping, to my eye, than an identical pair. Perfect symmetry can feel rigid, while easy harmony exudes comfort.

How lovely it would be to find perfect balance, and hold it still. Yet life is too dynamic for stasis; the unpredictable intrudes. With countless demands, we often teeter toward whatever claims our current attention, ever unsettled. So how do we gauge a balance of the heart? When we aim to find the internal fulcrum of our spiritual scale, our steady adjustments grow fluid. That golden standard indicates when our balance has shifted, so we can return to equipoise.

Unless proportion is considered, a decorative emphasis can easily be missed. On an entry wall, a small picture can be lost; a top-heavy shade dwarfs a small lamp; on a large table, a tiny accessory disappears. The eye is drawn to the open space, the larger shade, the flat expanse. Life works this way as well. Often we find our concentration on less-than-essential matters. How can we train our focus to attend to what matters most?

Proportion is our rationale for weighing the beautiful and functional, family and career commitments, the efficacious and efficient. The steady, well-proportioned progress of our days instills a calm self-possession. Trappist monk Thomas Merton writes that "happiness is not a matter of intensity, but of balance and order and rhythm and harmony." Achieving balance generates composure, assured acceptance, and the ability to deal with what confronts us. The poise which results demonstrates a sure sense of what is significant. ✄

Basic Black

B lack belongs. Black cording on a chair defines its lines. A black faux fur pillow, black sconce shades trimmed in jet beads, a wrought-iron candelabrum punctuate a space. In the garden, dark leaves emphasize bright blooms. In a wardrobe, black highlights a crisp white blouse, a bold cotton sweater, or pale linen slacks. Dark moments define life's brightness as well. If every day, joy followed joy, would we notice bliss? Limits distinguish our happiness. Dark moments make us recognize the measure of our joy. Like knots of a necklace, adversity distinguishes the beads of happiness.

Bees travel great distances to collect pollen, creating honey not only from beautiful flowers, but from weeds as well. We may find ourselves transported to far and unfamiliar fields of defeat, delay, or disillusionment, but the pain and heartache we encounter can be transformed to sweet elixir for the spirit.

In the dark of a summer evening, sensations are more acute than in the glare and glut of day. Scents rising from earth, stars piercing the heavens, moon-lit blossoms, breeze kissing skin are all more vivid because our senses are less distracted when heat and light have faded. Perception becomes more pronounced. Adversity, too, can heighten our reverence for what truly matters—our

spiritual life, our relationships with dear ones. In dimmer hours, we savor a more vivid resonance of heart. Thomas Carlyle draws our attentions to the heavens, where "the eternal stars shine out again, so soon as it is dark enough."

A close friend and professor colleague always presented upcoming tests to his classes as "opportunities."   He prompts me to consider life's tests as opportunities—to acquire knowledge, to gain skills, to hone abilities, to seek resources, to enhance understanding, to engage new challenges, and to cultivate the spirit. We will not make an A with every effort, but we will certainly learn and grow.

Boldness

"Boldness has genius, power, and magic in it," enthuses Johann Wolfgang von Goethe. The brilliance, vitality, and enchantment of a bold approach cannot always be defined, but it is easy to recognize. It provokes new ideas, ambition to pursue them, and unexpectedly exciting results.

Panache is a word I love, perhaps because it means a plume of feathers, one of my decorating signatures. Great vases of peacock and ostrich feathers punctuate our living room, gifts from my husband Michael. Panache also connotes dash and daring, essential elements of any design. The tentative and timid have no room in memorable style. Impressive design requires risk.

What enlivens a room? Choose your pizzazz. Perhaps you have a penchant for luscious color. A friend with flair lined her dining room in embossed wallpaper, and painted it a daring, sumptuous raspberry. In candlelight, her walls reflected an alluring blush in the faces of dinner guests. Instead of artificial (looking!) flowers, a bunch of willowy branches spritzed with gold and copper, arranged casually in a tall vase, can provide height and drama—for pennies. Begin with one dramatic element—a boldly patterned chair, an oversized garden urn unexpectedly indoors, a provocative painting, sumptuous yardage for theatrical draperies. Ease beyond inhibition into the realm of wow!

Fashion editor Carmel Snow defines elegance as "good taste plus a dash of daring," while designer Christian Dior holds that "zest is the secret of all beauty." Refinement assumes an exciting edge when embroidered with a bit of bold. A well-tailored outfit turns exuberant with a vivid shawl or striking oversized beads. Just a touch of flamboyance can turn simple to sass. Find your nerve; go for verve.

Landscapes, too, easily suffer from boredom. Yawning lawns, monotonous shrubs, and bland borders induce sleep in uninspired garden beds. Waking up outdoor rooms, just as indoor ones, requires emphasis. A great planter of perfumed flowers, a spectacular architectural tree, the stirring of a warbling fountain, a rough-textured stone path—all are perfect accents to enliven grounds and rouse the senses.

A German friend is a woman of great élan. She has a vibrant sense of fun and fashion. Her adored husband died unexpectedly, leaving her a young widow with his business affairs to manage, a household to run, and his mother to care for, all in addition to her own family and career to attend. Not long after his death, she invited me as a houseguest. Over late-night tea, she related the challenges of assuming so much her husband had always handled. "Believe me," she confided, "taking on a husband's responsibilities requires courage." She simply identified what needed to be done, learned as she went, and carried on in her indomitable way. Because her German apartment was small, without space for a guest room, I slept beside her in her husband's bed. All through the night, her bangle bracelets tinkled with silver music. Despite her loss, even in her sleep, her irrepressible spirit sang.

Often it is sheer pluck that compels us to overcome our challenges and hesitation. While visiting France during my new husband's military assignment in Europe, I made tentative efforts to speak French, weighing my vocabulary and sentence construction, aiming for correctness as we English professors are inclined to do. By the time I had my thoughts ordered and ready to deliver, I

OFTEN IT IS SHEER PLUCK THAT COMPELS US TO OVERCOME OUR CHALLENGES AND HESITATION.

found the conversational opportunity had long since moved on to other matters. Before our return visit, I was determined to gain competency in French and enrolled in classes with a lovely elderly French professor, who still recalled the privations of World War II, her bare legs chilblained as she walked to morning classes at the Sorbonne. Outside of class, I studied arduously with a nun from the college. Yet my efforts to learn language from books were never as effective as my husband's approach. He simply listened to conversation at nearby bistro tables, absorbed a handful of vocabulary, and plunged right in. No matter that he made errors—the point was trying. I followed his lead. French folks were always delighted by our attempts, encouraged us, and joined the collaboration to understand each other. Although our linguistic skills were limited, our communication succeeded through sheer audacity.

Henry David Thoreau encourages,"Go confidently in the direction of your dreams. Live the life you have imagined." Although I had aspired to authorship since childhood and had long taught college writing classes, I was hesitant to attempt book publishing. The enterprise seemed daunting. How many aspiring writers must exist? How few become published authors? But my passion to write also made me ask, "Why couldn't I be one of them?" Once I made the leap, enthusiasm carried me through the arduous undertaking to seeing my first book in print. Not only can doubt stand in our way of accomplishing what we might, but our dreams are often deterred by a lack of daring.

Fear motivates most of our mistakes and inhibitions. Because we fear being alone, we marry the wrong person; because we fear not having enough, we work long hours at the expense of family; because we fear discomfort, we avoid a new challenge; because we fear rejection, we avoid risking a new relationship; because we fear inadequacy, we fail to try; and because we fear the unknown, we ignore the voice of our heart. Eudora Welty contends that "all serious daring starts from within." Release fear's hold. Be bold!

What is the worst that can happen? The response to this question is often significantly less than our worry, dread, and anxious imagining. Will our feelings be hurt, our pride injured, our status diminished? Might we miss out? Will we have to begin again? How difficult is recovery from such wounds—really? Honestly considering the ultimate consequences of a choice can be liberating.

Each year, 11,243 injuries occur to people who are reading. We cannot avoid risk entirely, so why settle for safe when we could thrill with possibility? French author Colette gives permission: "You will do foolish things, but do them with enthusiasm." The word "enthusiasm" originates in the Greek, meaning "God in us." Ardor and abandon convey a transcendent spirit.

A few years ago, I lost a dear friend, a red-head full of snap and sparkle even in her 90s. Her walk to the dining hall of her retirement home was punctuated by visits with residents drawn to her vivacity. As her health failed, friends of all ages visited and contacted her. She had spent her life vigorously cultivating relationships. She visited, called, sent a note or flowers to those needing encouragement, wrote a helpful check to someone in need, cheered spirits with a compliment, introduced a profitable business contact, offered gentle guidance, created more good will than could be recounted, prompted smiles wherever she went, and had so much fun! Her enthusiasm for others constantly rekindled her spark, and lit her own life with a radiant brilliance. She shared the philosophy of Abraham Lincoln: "In the end, it's not the years in your life that count. It's the life in your years."

Celebration

When it comes to celebrating holidays, my husband Michael and I are rather unconventional. Some of our favorite holidays are less popular ones.

On February 2, we celebrate Candlemas, both a secular and religious holiday. In Christian tradition, Candlemas commemorates the Purification of the Virgin Mary, when Jesus was presented in the temple. Because a church's candle supply was blessed on this day for the year ahead, the holiday became known as Candlemas. Winter's midpoint, this first glimmer of spring is celebrated in many cultures, as in America's groundhog weather prediction. Michael and I enjoy the French tradition of eating crepes—golden round symbols of the sun. We turn lights low, light a fire in the fireplace, place shimmering candles all about the house, and spend a quiet evening in the company of friends or family. Guests luxuriate in the intimate stillness and always hope to be invited next year.

We have also imported the fun of April Fish from France. On April 1, confectioners offer chocolates, breads, and sweets in the shape of fish. As a little joke, French children attempt to tape a paper fish to the back of a friend without being noticed. In a Parisian bistro, we witnessed an adult version of the jest, confreres taping a wine coaster to the overcoat of an attorney friend. At home, we pull the prank on each other and leave paper fish in unlikely places—the freezer, underwear drawer, toothbrush holder, in a shoe, under a pillow, or in the ice bin. We carry the fish theme to serving seafood for dinner and salads in fish-shaped plates. Anything amusing is admitted.

May Day bears fond memories of hanging homemade baskets, decorated with colored paper and filled with flowers and candy. As children, we would ring the doorbells of friends, relatives, and teachers, then vanish, leaving our anonymous gifts at their doors. Today I still enjoy attaching an affectionate greeting to a small bouquet in this spring gesture of friendship.

For Kentucky Derby Day, we invite friends, hats encouraged, to watch the event with us. Recent British guests could not initially imagine the entertainment of watching a televised horse race, about which they knew nothing, but soon found themselves in the spirit of the day when mint juleps and "horse d'oeuvres" were served. Each drew a horse and cast a dollar bet. By post time, they were jumping and cheering for their horses along with the rest of the party. My husband's silly prizes contribute to the fun. First place wins the pot of money bets; for runners-up—horseradish, jockey shorts, a box of oats, horse cents (a small bag of pennies); and for the loser, glue (emblematic of equine doom).

One of our most memorable celebrations was for our parents' 50th wedding anniversary. At Sunday service, an ad hoc choir of family members, spouses, children—singers and non-singers— dedicated a hymn to our parents. That evening, we hosted an intimate family dinner. Seated in my sister's eat-in kitchen, the table extended and spread with a festive cloth, we bumped knees and elbows, enjoying the physical closeness of family ties. Children and grandchildren had been asked to bring a written piece to honor our parents—the verse of a song, a memory, a personal tribute, a quotation, or a poem. Some planned weeks in advance. Some wrote spontaneous, heartfelt lines.

Some could muster only a word or two. Others, including spouses of children, provided touching extemporaneous remarks or reminiscences.

The point of the evening was leisure. No rushing allowed. Simple multiple courses prepared ahead contributed to this easy pace and kept attention on the guests of honor. Each course was served and savored slowly, followed by words from a family member, read or recited. Throughout dinner, punctuating each course, everyone took a turn addressing our parents with personal remarks. Affectionate and moving messages, from even the youngest of grandchildren, soon prompted the passing of tissues. We are not by nature a particularly emotional or demonstrative family, but even the men among us were grateful for the circulating box. Once the tributes began, our initial reluctance gave way to an infectious desire to participate. We shared moments long treasured since childhood or lyrics that said what our own words could not. We laughed and cried in recognition and at each other. After the last bite of desert, we promised a special treat. On cue, from the living room wafted prerecorded strains of "Peg o' My Heart," my parents' song, played for them by a big band of the 1940s at their honeymoon hotel.

Long after the grand event, their anniversary dinner is fondly recalled not only by my parents, but by every participant. The evening remains a treasured gift of affection to resonate through the years.

Leo Tolstoy suggests that "the purpose of life is to express love in all its manifestations," so why wait to entertain until we can do so luxuriously? If we aim to make the occasion perfect, the day will never arrive. How often have we intended to invite those friends for dinner? Make a hearty soup, buy some crusty breads, and splash store-bought ice-cream with frozen strawberries for dessert. Guests who ask what they can bring may contribute an appetizer, salad, or

SHOULDN'T THE THINGS

WE LOVE MOST BE THE THINGS

WE USE MOST OFTEN?

bottle of wine. Create a festive mood with a jazzy tablecloth and pretty flowers. How hard can it be? When entertaining is easy, we will want to do it more often. Entertaining is first and primarily about getting people together. Guests will not remember what we served; they will recount the fond company and memories made.

In the words of Susan B. Anthony, "Sooner or later we all discover that the most important moments in life are not the advertised ones, not the birthdays, the graduations, the weddings, not the great goals achieved. The real milestones are less prepossessing. They come to the door of memory unannounced, stray dogs that amble in, sniff around a bit, and simply never leave. Our lives are measured by these."

Celebrations need not be dictated by calendar or special occasion. Every day, something commonplace, mundane, or ordinary can be enriched with attractive and meaningful touches. An acquaintance with beautiful collections keeps all her best wares in basement boxes, where they are too much bother to retrieve. Shouldn't the things we love most be the things we use most often? Maybe fragile crystal is too risky for everyday beverages, but a wine glass could hold flowers snipped from the garden. For whom are we saving our best? Why not leave a legacy of living? Leigh Hunt remarks that "the most fascinating women are those that can most enrich the everyday moments of existence."

CELEBRATIONS NEED NOT BE DICTATED BY CALENDAR OR SPECIAL OCCASION.

On our kitchen table is a vintage tablecloth, roses with art deco detail in careful cross-stitch. Found in pristine condition among my great aunt's hope-chest treasures, it is too precious to worry about stains and repeated laundering. The solution? I have covered it with glass cut to table-top size. Special keepsakes need not be hands-off. With a little imagination, they can offer regular pleasure.

Each day offers reason for celebrating, and being the subject of a toast is always a thrill. Toasts, even with non-alcoholic beverages, are a happy way to thank a dear one for a simple favor or an everyday kindness. Toast a child for cleaning his room without being asked, a husband for filling the car with gasoline and saving you the trip, a friend for recommending a great novel. Thoughtfulness is always worth celebrating. A lovely toast to a beloved when enjoying a glass of wine together comes from Song of Solomon 4:10 *(NKJV)*: "How much better than wine is your love."

Comfort

"To be happy at home is the ultimate result of all ambition, the end to which every enterprise and labor tends." Samuel Johnson articulates how we feel about the comfort of home. Home is our respite, our repose, our renewal. When we depend on home for so much, we want to love being there. What makes a home hospitable? To begin with, comfortable furniture on which even the dog is allowed. Simply cover his favorite spot with an inexpensive throw and hide lint brushes in every room. Arrange chairs in easy conversational groupings. Provide places to put up one's feet, to set glasses. Forget the spindly coffee-table; instead, cover a large ottoman in faux leather. Place a great reading chair near a sunlit window with plenty of books nearby.

For many of us, formal rooms are wasted space, rarely used. Turn a formal living room into a family space with generous shelving. Omit the television, but make room for a library and computers. Instead of isolating themselves in bedrooms, children can socialize, and parents can monitor computer use. Install a large table for homework or reading the paper, for children's games and family projects. Include a cushy divan for lounging or cuddling with the cat. When rooms are inviting, people will want to gather there.

In the wardrobe, comfort is often misinterpreted. Legendary designer Coco Chanel liberated fashion from corsets, stays, and petticoats to suit women's increasingly active lifestyles—short skirts, simple sheaths, unstructured knits, cardigans, pleated skirts, trousers, belted men's jackets and sweaters, shoulder bags, costume jewelry, and bobbed hair. Her mission and ambition were simple, comfortable design for freedom and function.

Unfortunately, the principle of comfort has devolved in recent decades. Comfortable means feeling at home with one's best appearance; it does not mean careless and unkempt. If drawers

are filled with sloppy tees, shapeless sweatshirts, scruffy shorts, and shabby jeans, the temptation to schlep and slouch is too easy. Recycle unflattering apparel at the thrift shop. Okay, reserve a piece or two for house cleaning and garden chores. Otherwise, conveniently place those attractive pieces you have been reserving for special occasions, and wear them! As you gradually improve your look, seek flattering and easy-to-wear clothing additions, which complement items you already own. Any of Chanel's suggestions are classics of style. Many stores offer helpful wardrobe advice for enhancing individual size, shape, age, and activity as well. Comfort can be compatible with chic.

Contrary to what shoe designers would lead us to believe, footwear need not hurt to be fashionable. Because finding moderately priced shoes which are both stylish and comfortable can be like seeking the Holy Grail, a trip to the shoe repair shop is one of the best steps feet can take. An expert can ease, stretch, pad, support, and shape shoes to a personal fit. Your feet will thank you

An important component of comfort is order. In fact, Pearl S. Buck insists that "order is the shape on which beauty depends." Consider the well-stocked pantry, an organized closet, tidy drawers, conveniently arranged rooms, a manageable schedule, an uncluttered desk. How much more efficient and pleasant order can make our days. Confusion and disarray make us feel agitated and unsettled. Organization and structure convey harmony and decorum. Once established, order is easier to maintain than to impose when chaos has crept in and engulfed us. If life seems out of order, we can restore comfort by clearing the mess, one drawer at a time. As Alexander Pope observes, "Order is Heaven's first law."

Ease accompanies order. Examining our own values can help us to loosen up, to avoid the dictates of society which do not apply to us—the contrived conformity, obligations, proprieties, and suspect influences, stressing ourselves for luxuries mistaken for essentials. When we are comfortable with our own choices, we find priorities ordered, and life falls into place. We discover time to give undivided attention to a loved one, to linger with a child at bedtime, to sing, to pray, to read, to recount blessings, or to squeeze each other. Such sweet delights are life's truest luxuries . . . and comforts.

> WHEN WE ARE COMFORTABLE WITH OUR OWN CHOICES, WE FIND PRIORITIES ORDERED, AND LIFE FALLS INTO PLACE.

Confidence

"IN QUIETNESS AND IN CONFIDENCE SHALL BE YOUR STRENGTH" (Isaiah 30:15b, *KJV*).

When discontent raises its head, I am often reminded of one of my favorite childhood stories from a well-thumbed book, whose title and author I regret that my searches cannot locate nor my memory recall. (I would be indebted if a reader might help me to identify its source.) Here is how I remember the story, with apologies that it may bear loose resemblance to the original after so many years:

A small brown pony admired the beautiful horses pastured near him. Oh, what he would give to be yellow like the palomino or spotted like the appaloosa. The little pony thought that any color would be better than his own plain brown.

He lay in a field, very still, hoping rays of sunlight might turn his coat to gold. Though he basked for hours, he remained the same brown pony. He went for a swim in the pond, hoping the sky's reflection on water might turn him blue. But when he emerged, he was only wet, his ears dripping slimy moss. He rolled in the lush grass, hoping to turn green, back and forth, back and forth, but he only grew dizzy.

One day he saw the farmer painting his barn. When the farmer left for the day, the little brown pony rubbed his sides against that beautiful red paint. How pleased he was with his new red coat! But soon his skin began to sting. He rolled in the grass and swam in the pond, but he could not remove the paint. His skin burned like fire. Finally, the farmer saw the little pony's uncomfortable plight. He washed the pony with a smelly soap, rinsed him clean, and brushed him till he shone.

The pony felt so much better and went for a drink in the pond. There he saw the reflection of a beautiful brown pony. How happy he was to be himself again!

Thank you to the author of that tale, which made such a childhood impression.

When we bought our first home after many years of military moves, we found flooring and walls in need of updating. I visited home-improvement stores so often that I was soon greeted by name. The choices were overwhelming. After living in military quarters, where choice was not an option, I was not prepared for an entire store devoted to wall paper. Mind-numbing days of browsing, toting home samples, debating and dithering followed. Finally, I settled on embossed faux-tile wallpaper for the Old World look I desired in the kitchen. My paper hanger, however, was less than enthused at my request to apply it both above counters and as wainscoting in the dining area. Before she could convince me to change my mind, I stuck to my tired-of-looking guns, and asked her to proceed. Seeing the finished results, we were both pleased. My well-considered instincts often serve me best; I ignore them at my own peril.

When confronted by options and opinions, we can become confused or swayed. But too much indecision and second-guessing are paralyzing. And often, well-intentioned advice can stifle enthusiasm altogether. We can easily be dissuaded and inclined to rationalize inaction. Decorating decisions may not be so consequential, but measuring our significant choices by what we value most and holding to those standards can facilitate decision and clarify our judgment. The words of Euripides are valid still: "There is just one life for each of us: our own."

Why is saying "no" so difficult? We want to decline and stand
our ground, yet to avoid hurt feelings. To refuse politely but firmly,
we might respond, "No," but express our thanks; "No," but offer
another possibility; "No," and shift the subject; "No" and "No" again
for emphasis; or my husband's confident favorite, "No," period. As
fashion editor Diana Vreeland asserts, "Elegance is refusal."

NEW CHALLENGES WILL NOT BECOME EASIER IMMEDIATELY, BUT FACILITY WILL DEVELOP OVER TIME.

We gain confidence not only by recognizing and adhering to our own divinely instilled standards of behavior, but also by embracing the uncomfortable, the difficult. New challenges will not become easier immediately, but facility will develop over time. Persisting in our tasks and doing them well instill confidence. If we just continue pedaling, regardless how distant the goal ahead may seem, when we finally reach the summit and glance behind, we find proficiency has been seated tandem all along. Winston Churchill cheers us on: "Success is not final, failure is not fatal: it is the courage to continue that counts."

Contrast

Nothing enlivens like contrast. Dark and light distinguish each other. Ivory walls dramatize stimulating art. Pale carpet highlights carved antique wood. In a shady garden, bright blooms draw attention.

Simple paired with opulent emphasizes the inherent qualities of each. In a crystal punchbowl, my husband's baseball collection juxtaposes a signed Mickey Mantle with scuffed sandlot keepsakes from childhood. A richly embroidered velvet cushion accents a chair in simple linen. A gilded statue perches on a provincial soda-fountain table. Contradiction punctuates both stately and humble.

New invigorates old. Antique tapestry chairs converse with a contemporary table; a season's most fashionable accessories add punch to classic pants and jackets; fresh linens illumine grandmother's china.

Plain spotlights fancy. Pearls pair unpredictably with a tee shirt; sparkle shakes up chambray; a casual jacket partners improbably with a floaty silk skirt; heels give jeans an unlikely kick.

Unexpected differences inject interest, impose definition, and spark levity. Mix metaphors—elegant and easy; refined and relaxed; sophisticated and surprising; formal and fanciful; precious, plebeian, and playful. Contrast animates. As John Locke phrases the optimum tension, "That which is static and repetitive is boring. That which is dynamic and random is confusing. In between lies art."

As a host, my husband Michael often conducts creative social choreography, mingling old friends and new, urbane and rustic, young and old, reticent and outrageous, adept and inept, conservative and flamboyant. His compositions require courage as these parties tend to take on lives of their own. Despite my misgivings, however, unlikely dynamics energize our entertaining. Ben Johnson expresses my husband's attitude when he says, "All concord's born of contraries."

Life is complex, uncertain, paradoxical. In this world, contradictions are seldom reconciled. We will feel more content if we can recognize that incongruities coexist—and not always peaceably. What is important, advises former Radcliffe College President Martina Horner, is "to keep learning, to enjoy challenge, and to tolerate ambiguity. In the end there are no certain answers."

Conversation

Home serves many of our most fundamental needs, including protection, warmth, nurturing, and society. Home, our first society, establishes a necessary sense of belonging. As our primary medium of social exchange, conversation knits relationships at home and in the larger world. Among the skills transmitted to children, the essentials of communication are invaluable. Ralph Waldo Emerson claims, "The best of life is conversation."

Before technology, we had time for poignant pauses, pondering ideas, and pleasures of conversation. On Sundays as a child, I listened to my mother and aunts talk as they worked together in my grandfather's kitchen. Later in the evening around a great oak table, in chats overheard, I learned about family and life. Though neither monumental nor inspired, these common visits modeled the etiquette, tempo, and nuance of dialogue and introduced me to the rich rewards of conversation. The art is worth mastering. Through human discourse, which Homer calls "the sweeter banquet of the mind," we create intimacy and navigate the world.

Talk today is booming, in what often seems pointless drivel. When I reach for recent examples of satisfying conversation, I find them scarce. Exchanges tend to skim along the superficial surface of multiple topics at a disconcerting staccato. As I consider a speaker's remarks, and mull an interjection or response, the moment for reply is often lost as more talk rushes to fill the void. Conversation requires a leisure which speakers often seem unwilling to extend.

So what constitutes a good conversationalist? To begin with, a good conversationalist listens carefully. After all, what can one learn while talking? Listening indicates that we value the speaker and what she is saying. Paul Tillich admonishes, "The first duty of love is to listen." This obligation means being attentive, looking directly at the speaker, avoiding distraction, focusing intently on the person talking, without speaking or interrupting to shift the focus to ourselves, without thinking ahead to our response, without anticipating or discounting the importance of what is being said and tuning out. By listening for clues, we sense when to expand on a subject, to shift in a new direction, or to pass the ball. Listening requires time and care, but pays great dividends in drawing us closer, improving our confidences, and deepening our relationships.

A good conversationalist speaks thoughtfully and asks provocative questions, trying to elicit what interests the listener. Dialogue is the aim of conversation, not monopoly . . . or monotony. Reciprocated interest keeps a discourse lively and satisfying to both parties.

A good conversationalist avoids criticism and complaint. Criticism damages, while grumbling infects with gloom and discontent. Of course, we may share concerns among our intimacies, but we want to avoid wallowing in them. Good conversationalists exude gratitude and good cheer.

A good conversationalist praises specifically and sincerely. We all thrive on recognition and affirmation.

A good conversationalist seeks the opinions of others, is sensitive to differing views, applies tact in expressing her own ideas, and promotes courteous disagreement.

A good conversationalist injects timely topics to keep talk lively. She offers convivial company and informed, intelligent exchange with a zest of wit.

OTHERS WILL RETAIN LITTLE OF THE CONTENT WE CONVEY IN CONVERSATION, BUT THEY WILL LONG REMEMBER HOW WE MADE THEM FEEL.

Others will retain little of the content we convey in conversation, but they will long remember how we made them feel. Henry David Thoreau describes the pleasure: "The greatest compliment that was ever paid to me was when one asked me what I thought, and attended to my answer."

And let us not neglect our most vital and intimate conversations, those we have with God, who listens intently to even wordless expressions of the heart. The more often we speak with God, the more clearly we recognize His always perfect response. The words of Ralph Waldo Emerson ring true: "No one ever prayed without learning something."

Curve

"The grace of a curve is an invitation to remain. We cannot break away from it without hoping to return," notes French philosopher Gaston Bachelard. The sinuous line of a crystal vase, the sweeping bend of a garden lane, the elegant turn of a cabriole leg, a neckline's soft inflection, the lithe incline of tulips—curves have a fluid way of easing a glance. While rigid lines command the eye, flowing turns, loose spirals, winding curls allow for visual meandering. We are slowed and suspended as grace reveals itself. The Earth herself has few straight lines, and how can we improve on nature's gentle undulations? Mae West, famous for her voluptuous figure, defines a curve as "the loveliest distance between two points."

When the sharp angles of relationships make us edgy, we may incline toward being straightforward, but approaching indirectly with the graceful curves of courtesy can keep us from injuring ourselves or harming others on life's hard edges. As Cicero observes, "Whatever is graceful is virtuous, and whatever is virtuous is graceful."

Detail

If life is in the details, we want the minutiae to be meaningful. Our whatnots, bibelots, trifles and trinkets are more than embellishment; they are a heart's expression. Johann Wolfgang von Goethe reflects, "We are shaped and fashioned by what we love."

Favorite books, family photographs, art work, and travel mementos make a home our own. Anyone can fill a room with furnishings and decorative objects perfectly coordinated from a retail store, but rooms gain interest from personal inflections. Spaces appear evolved rather than decorated. The value of our accumulations is in their stories— a tarnished statue of Joan of Arc from an afternoon spent making friends in France, the annotated literature book of a beloved aunt who inspired me to teach, an etching from our favorite overlook of Heidelberg's castle, a mended crochet tablecloth from my grandparents' bedside. None of these items would seem to have anything in common, but I believe that if we love an object, it will go with anything else we love. Rather than matching style or color, the link is our affection. Treasured details give home a personal signature. Coco Chanel's adage applies: "Adornment is never anything except a reflection of the heart."

A guest could not have known how her comment delighted me when she described our home as "sensuous." To create a space we love, where friends want to come, I make a distinct effort to appeal to the senses—aged wood, soft lamp light, old tapestry, and sumptuous upholstery. I want rooms to feel indulgent, comfortable, and a little flirtatious, by injecting hints of silk, scented flowers, female form, soft jazz, flickering candles, and delicate table legs dancing across a polished floor. The seductive allure is an invitation to linger. Oscar Wilde expresses the delight of detail: "Now and then it is a joy to have one's table red with wine and roses."

Have you noticed how the pigment in your cat's eyes resembles the endpapers of vintage books? Can you taste summer flowers in morning's golden honey? When did you last snuggle the scent of your husband's clean-shaven face or stroke the warm cornsilk of your daughter's sunlit hair? If we could heighten our senses to perceive life's smallest graces, we would bask in gratitude. For, as Harvard minister and professor Peter Gomes maintains, "It is beauty that affirms the presence of God."

Economy

As a writer, I understand the importance of economy, editing lines for succinct impact. In most applications, less truly is more. A stunning specimen of jewelry shows best with few competing pieces. Decorative treasures shine in uncluttered rooms. Limiting variety in garden plants increases visual impact. Restraint renders us more cognizant, more appreciative than excess. French moralist Joseph Joubert asserts, "Of what delights are we deprived by our excesses!"

Saturday garage sales seem a peculiar institution to others with whom we share the globe. Why do Americans buy so much that they do not need, discard it, and keep acquiring more? Why do we feel compelled to gratify our immediate cravings with poor choices, never to feel satisfied? We might blame our greed on advertising creating excessive desires, but why do we succumb to the seduction? Think about impulse purchases. If an expenditure still seems necessary a week later, we can usually return for it. This interlude is a surprisingly easy way to sort needs from wants.

Americans consume far more than our share of the world's resources. Considering our impact on the earth may help us to think small. With conscious choices, soon our personal acts of conservation will begin to feel more fulfilling than waste. Henry David Thoreau expresses the benefit of economy this way: "A man is rich in proportion to the things he can afford to leave alone."

"Making do" was a common expression in our household while we were growing up, although the term is seldom employed today. Buying new made no sense when what we already had was still serviceable. "Making do" is more than an expression; it is a philosophy that still motivates my conservation.

Most of the curtains in our house, in adaptable ivory, have been hemmed, unhemmed, cut, resewn, and adjusted in a variety of incarnations to fit widely fluctuating window sizes in a series of military and civilian quarters. . . . For a striking table centerpiece, I have arranged snippings of sweet autumn clematis from a neighborhood ditch, gladioli from an aging bouquet, and peace lilies from a houseplant, with purple cuttings of American beauty berry, wandering jew, and sweet potato vine from the yard in a graceful soup tureen. . . . An inexpensive bottle of bay rum from the barber supply store makes a spicy after-bath splash. . . . A favorite floral skirt has been getting updates for years, shortened, lengthened, recut, and remade.

I have inherited frugality, another antiquated term, from my mother. Why, I wonder, does she not replace the pots and pans with which she set up housekeeping sixty years ago, warped from cooking innumerable meals, beaten by children in the sand pile? Yet now I find myself unable to toss my own pans, starting to tip, too. After all, my mother's voice echoes in my own, "They still heat." My mother and Euripides agree: "Enough is abundance to the wise."

Anyone can look like a million bucks . . . if she has a million bucks, but the fun is in looking good with more art than money. Dressing well requires much less than we are led to believe. We will never regret investing in high quality basics—well-fitting skirts and pants with classic lines in neutral colors that can be worn for years. As seasonal styles change, blouses, tops, and sweaters can easily freshen a wardrobe with minor expense. Buying clothes that do not require commercial dry cleaning cuts costs further . . . and who wants cleaning chemicals near her skin anyway? Not only are washable natural fibers a healthier, more economical choice than synthetics, but nature's own textures are incomparably beautiful.

How many acquisitions are truly invaluable? How many acquaintances make real contributions to our wellbeing? How many activities crowding our days are truly necessary? To pare clutter from life, start small. Begin by canceling catalogs—saving time, trees, and temptation. Then move to drawers, closets, and the garage. Be ruthless. Recycle discards with a local charity. Next, start on the calendar and "to do" list. Scratch off non-essentials. Clearing room allows the spirit to expand into those open spaces.

Now, most importantly, pledge not to acquire another single item or obligation unless it is essential or worthwhile. Training ourselves to find pleasure in ignoring our cravings means negotiating a balance between sufficiency and surfeit. If we need incentive, we might consider all the natural resources we are preserving when fewer unnecessary goods are produced, all the personal delights of freer hours. If we are racing and acquiring to find fulfillment, can we shift pursuit of appetites to more enduring satisfactions?

How MANY ACQUISITIONS ARE TRULY INVALUABLE?

British reformer Joseph Brotherton remarks, "My riches consist not in the extent of my possessions but in the fewness of my wants." Some desires may be worthy, but consumption never fills us, and what is neglected in the chase? Frugality frees us. We have less maintenance, worry, debt, and stress. We become more available, more attentive, more engaged.

The world is full of wealthy people who amassed their fortunes by saving instead of spending, keeping out of debt, living in modest homes, driving used cars, being reasonable about extras. But the greatest dividends of small appetites come in richer relationships with ourselves, our God, our dear ones. As Cicero states, "To be content with what we possess is the greatest and most secure of riches."

Ephemera

E ighteenth century American women decorated their hair with fireflies. Gentlewomen of an earlier century wore treasured gloves spun from spider webs. What frivolities could be more fleeting . . . or more breathtaking? John Ruskin comments on ephemeral pleasures: "Remember that the most beautiful things in the world are the most useless; peacocks and lilies for instance."

Perhaps its transience is among the reasons I am so enamored of scent, our neglected sense. I read and write about the subject and immerse myself in fragrant revels at every opportunity— dishes infused with garlic and herbs, spicy curries, perfume redolent of pepper or myrrh, berry bouquets of wine, our cat's fur after her morning ablutions, spring garden soil, an autumn attar of decaying leaves. Such ecstasies cannot be saved to relish later. Their trailing traces are meant to seize.

Cut flowers, the ultimate ephemera, remain a timeless gift of gratitude and affection. Their fleeting luxury never fails to delight. A bit beyond uninspired supermarket bunches, small arrangements with creative flair are often available from neighborhood florists. Even on a limited budget, a single extraordinary stem can be an exquisite gift. Late in the week, perishable overstock may be available at reduced prices. When bringing flowers to a hostess, do remember to bring them arranged, preserving her precious time with guests.

Ephemera can easily be incorporated into decorating. In a scarred
frame, chipping its copper paint, I have replaced a dark oil still-life
with mirror to brighten our kitchen. The change has transformed
the lifeless space into a shining backdrop for fun ephemera. We
post magazine clippings, photographs, phrases, snippets of verse
that speak to us at the moment or make us laugh. Currently, we
are marveling or giggling at Joe Namath in his slippers, robe, and
smile; a pair of women's legs in platform shoes crossed in the sun
of a car window; a Frenchman tipping his chair in a café doorway;
a crouching cougar; poetry of Ted Kooser; a battlefield funeral
service; children skinny dipping; a Frida Kahlo postcard; the Paris
Opera staircase; a woman and her daughter in red riding capes
driving a convertible through a wolf-infested forest; Cole Porter
lyrics; a golden mermaid; and laughing French ham purveyors. The
changing collage reminds us that life is
composed of snapshots—unrelated,
elusive moments that will never be
recaptured. Instants are insistent.
Illuminating flashes catch the
fragile present and reflect its
lingering grace. Poet e. e.
cummings artfully reminds
us of the momentary
pleasures worth seizing:
"though love be a day and life
be nothing, it shall not stop
kissing."

Faith

"NOW FAITH IS BEING SURE OF WHAT WE HOPE FOR AND CERTAIN OF WHAT WE DO NOT SEE" (Hebrews 11:1).

A friend who grew up in Germany and suffered the privations following World War II recalls her father's attentions to his small aquarium of fish. Feeding and watching them seemed a quiet distraction over which he had some control when so much else in the world had been turned upside down. Because they had no heat in the apartment overnight, her father would rise on frosty mornings to break the water's icy surface, faithfully greeting and feeding his fish. One bitter dawn, our friend recalls waking from freezing sleep to find her father in tears. His fish had died, and with their loss, her father's frail hold on normalcy had frozen, too.

Our hope is buffeted daily. The chill of despair can seem beyond thaw. Hope can be precarious, but it is also tenacious. When the worst arrives, and it will, even a glimmer of faith radiates heat enough to slowly warm us once more. "Faith," says Rabindranath Tagore, "is the bird that feels the light and sings when the dawn is still dark." A beloved English proverb comforts us with the reminder that "God tempers the wind to the shorn lamb." He will adjust assaults to our capacity for handling them.

Despite our awareness that God is in command, how hard it is to give up control! Despite white-knuckles, detours, and second-guessing, we insist on remaining in the driver's seat. Yet even Christ himself recognized a greater wisdom, submitting His ultimate destiny to God. He taught us to pray, "Your will be done on earth as it is in heaven" (Matthew 6:10). When we recognize that God's perfect plan will always be in our own best interest, we can relinquish the steering wheel to more capable hands and free ourselves to discover new avenues of blessing. To change drivers, all we need to do is release our grip, slide over, and feel the wind in our hair.

Abraham Lincoln expresses the indispensable comfort of faith: "I have been driven many times upon my knees, by the overwhelming conviction that I had nowhere else to go. My own wisdom and that of all about me seemed insufficient for that day." No matter how carefully we design our lives, we must finally abandon our best efforts to faith. Fortunes fluctuate, bright days dim, relationships strain, health suffers, dear ones depart. Eventually, all in life will be discontinued, even our favorite lipstick, especially our favorite lipstick, so stock up now on the enduring essentials—faith, hope, and love—in every conceivable shade.

Faith depends not only on our ability to look ahead, but also on our ability to look behind to evidence of past providence. This dual perspective can remove fear, renew strength, revive desire, restore spirit, and engage us in new challenges. In the words of Mother Teresa, "We must never get into the habit of being preoccupied with the future. There is no reason to do so. God is there."

Food

"One cannot think well, love well, sleep well, if one has not dined well," writes Virginia Woolf. Because food is so vital, it deserves more thoughtful attention than it often receives.

When my husband and I begin to salivate at the very thought of their fragrant crimson delight, we head to local growers for strawberries ripe from the vine. Later, in our own yard, a fig tree's bounty proclaims summer official. Because we cannot bear to see such abundance wasted, I conquer the ubiquitous harvest in muffins and tortes. With goat cheese, walnuts, and honey, figs serve as lovely salad. With prosciutto and mustard cream, they make a fine finale. We eat figs and more figs, until we could sprout the proverbial fig leaves that clothed our infamous ancestors. Finally, when the last litter is sticky with bees beneath the tree, we turn to roadside peaches, dressed in sunset hues, and savor sweet beauty at summer's end.

Eating seasonally means enjoying foods at peak ripeness and flavor. Produce harvested and sold nearby has not been picked hard and tasteless to ship across continents. We may not always have time or

resources to rely solely on nearby provision, but seeking fresh resources and getting acquainted with local food purveyors of all kinds for meat,

℮ATING SEASONALLY

MEANS ENJOYING

FOODS AT PEAK

RIPENESS AND FLAVOR.

game, eggs, produce, organic products, and wholesome baked goods; seeking specialists who care about quality, taste, and healthfulness of food they raise and procure is worth the effort. Healthy foods are flavorful foods, seasonal and varied, as close to their original state and source as possible. Michael Pollan offers sound advice: "Eat food. Not too much. Mostly vegetables." "Don't eat anything that your great-grandmother wouldn't recognize as food."

Fresh foods bear no resemblance to those processed with refined sugars and artificial flavors. For a sublime breakfast, snack, or dessert, I plop fresh berries or fruit slices into plain yogurt and drizzle with pure maple syrup. Wholesome, flavorful food also deserves slow, attentive savoring. I happen to agree with John Gunther, who says, "All happiness depends on a leisurely breakfast."

Inquiring friends want to know why my refrigerated parsley wears a shower cap. I am indulging my parsley in spa treatment—feet in a shallow water bath, locks cuffed loosely in a plastic bag to moisten and aerate. It can bask for weeks in its cold resort, emerging fresh and invigorated. A handful of parsley or other fresh herbs revives even a humdrum dish as though it has just enjoyed a pampered vacation.

Other foods thrive in a warmer climate. A vine-ripened tomato, creamy brie, and rosy pear are all more delectable at room temperature. Enhance taste by taking off the chill. Food in its happiest state simply tastes better.

Tasteless food cannot satisfy our physical hunger or our sensory cravings. Like much else in life, consuming more will never content our innate desires. If we can accurately identify our appetites, by training our awareness, our pleasures will be richer, and a small amount of excellent quality will suffice. Hardy, easy-to-grow herbs contribute incomparable flavor. Those which die back in winter can be chopped and frozen in ice cube trays, covered in water. When thawed and drained, they bring the essence of summer to any dish any time of the year.

The sensory experience of natural food is one of life's most tantalizing satisfactions. "Nothing would be more tiresome than eating and drinking if God had not made them a pleasure as well as a necessity," says Voltaire. Texture, color, scent, sound, and taste all influence our appetite. What could improve the earthy aroma of beets, the crunch of tart apple, or the bright burst of juicy orange?

But eating naturally also means overlooking imperfections. Produce at farmers' markets may be odd shaped, off color, or bug bitten. Insisting on perfect beauty in food suggests that sight is the only sense that matters. Are a few blemishes really more disturbing than the chemical poisons of fertilizers and pesticides?

The further food is removed from its original state—refined, preserved, polluted, artificially flavored, colored, chemically altered, genetically modified, antibiotic infused, hormone-enhanced—the less healthful it can be. What is a Cheeto anyway? Its puffed florescence resembles nothing in the natural world. Eating better is easy—trade processed foods and long lists of ingredients for fresh fare, simply prepared with love. Wendell Berry advocates eating as close to food's natural state as possible, to taste and experience food as it was intended: "Better than any argument is to rise at dawn and pick dew-wet berries in a cup." Can't you just taste them?

Despite the pleasures of food, preparing meals is not always a favorite activity. Some evenings when cooking feels a chore, I turn for inspiration to a cookbook given to me by my husband. His inscription quotes Thomas Wolfe: "There is no spectacle on earth more appealing than that of a beautiful woman in the act of cooking dinner for someone she loves." It helps to remember that food preparation is a gift and a grace.

Preparing food need not be an elaborate undertaking. Even hungry children can retrieve ingredients, help with simple recipe steps, set a table, or draw artful placemats. Quiet music at this busy hour will also have a calming effect on insistent appetites, setting a leisurely stage for tranquil mealtime.

Food writer M. F. K. Fisher says, "Sharing food with another human being is an intimate act that should not be indulged in lightly." Mindful eating not only tastes good, it feels good. Gulping while electronics blare or while dashing to activities thwarts the pleasure of food and precious moments with dear ones. Meals are time for slowing the tempo and engaging with each other. Thoughtful conversation complements taste. The family dinner table is a sacred place for sharing thoughts and fellowship, for intimate communion. Julia Child praises the experience: "Dining with one's friends and beloved family is certainly one of life's primal and most innocent delights, one that is both soul-satisfying and eternal."

Fragrance

" I f the day and night are such that you greet them with joy, and life emits a fragrance like sweet-scented herbs, is more elastic, more starry, more immortal,—that is your success." I love Henry David Thoreau's fragrant analogy.

Just beyond our bedroom, an effusive wall of jasmine induces dusk delirium. With its sensual teasing and amorous intentions, it creeps through windows while we sleep. Open windows are the most natural way to invite fragrance indoors. Window boxes or planters outside a doorway can be filled with fragrant favorites. Or one can cool and freshen a room with scented breezes by misting lightweight or net curtains with herb-scented water—lavender, lemon verbena, vetiver—made from natural essential oils.

Personal fragrance is among the most intimate of expressions. It should reflect oneself truly. To enhance fragrance selection, the neglected sense of smell can be refined with visits to florists, wine tastings, nurseries, and fresh markets. Heightening awareness of aromas helps to identify scents which resonate personally—orange zest, cantaloupe, nutmeg, heliotrope, tobacco, or incense. These preferences are components to seek in fragrances for wearing. Personal scent should, first of all, delight oneself. For perfume is defined by French master perfumer Edmond Roudnitska as "an act of poetic thought."

One of my favorite ways to wear personal fragrance is scented jewelry. By tucking a cotton ball spritzed with perfume into a jewelry box, (careful that jewelry surfaces are not dampened), bracelets, beads, and earrings will waft a private allure. After all, as Karl Lagerfeld points out, "Perfume is provocation." I also like to layer a body cream beneath perfume. Unscented lotions infused with a few drops of one's own fragrance can also add a rich dimension to scent and make it linger.

Fragrant soaps are a delicious way to infuse a home with scent. I like the distinctive—black pepper, honey, anise, Italian gardens, and Spanish moss. Scented soaps are not only aromatic when lathered, but can scent a powder room while lounging in the soap dish. They can be tucked among towels and linens or into a lingerie drawer as well.

Scent is not incidental for me; it is requisite. Growing culinary herbs, seeking naturally scented candles, insisting on ambrosial tree-ripened peaches, finding a favorite perfume that expresses who I am— these are pursuits of pleasure, worth the effort. I share Vigil's desire: "Give me handfuls of lilies to scatter."

I want to cultivate fragrant delight. I want bedside bouquets more often. I want to draw deeply the scent of my husband's neck. I want cooking essences to tempt guests to our table and invite them to linger. I want to be vulnerable and receptive to unexpected and fleeting allures wafting my way. I want to cultivate a more attentive, sentient self.* Like Ralph Waldo Emerson, "I wish that life should not be cheap, but sacred, I wish the days to be as centuries, loaded, fragrant."

Lost ardor, misplaced memories, fragile bonds, transitory pleasures, forgotten delights, elusive peace . . . with a soft infusion of scent, life's sense of significance can be restored in a breath. In *Remembrance of Things Past*, Marcel Proust captures how aromas can conjure distant memories: "When from a long-distant past nothing subsists, after the people are dead, after the things are broken and scattered, taste and smell alone, more fragile but more enduring, more unsubstantial, more persistent, more faithful, remain poised a long time, like souls, remembering, waiting, hoping, amid the ruins of all the rest; and bear unflinchingly, in the tiny and almost impalpable drop of their essence, the vast structure of recollection."

An essence emits the odors of plants or substances from which it was extracted. It contains the inherent, indispensable properties which identify a scent. The essence of our personal selves is the intrinsic spiritual entity we exude, which defines our nature. We want that essence to be pure and highly refined, "for we are unto God the aroma of Christ" (2 Corinthians 2:15a).

*Adapted from "A Sense of Significance," previously published in *Sass*, May 2005.

Generosity

It comforted sick beds, swaddled dolls, muffled giggles, sunbathed in grass, costumed homespun dramas, and snuggled slumber parties. Mother's handmade quilt, a wedding gift from her mother-in-law, lived a colorful life. Like all of Mother's possessions, it was never tucked away in a trunk for posterity, but freely shared and well-used by a houseful of children. The quilt's once vibrant design is now faded and worn to its batting, but the memories it warmed are indelible. Diane Ackerman expresses the desire to mine the riches of our days: "I don't want to get to the end of my life and find that I lived just the length of it. I want to have lived the width of it as well."

A "lagniappe" is a Creole term of Southern Louisiana for an unexpected extra, bonus gift, or benefit, often from a merchant, but used in other applications. A dozen beignets, New Orleans' traditional donut confections, include one sugary extra. Perhaps the sweetest surprises are small kindnesses which anticipate the needs of another. My husband Michael is an artist at such thoughtfulness—leaving me the exact change for a highway toll, folding clothes I have left in the dryer, adding pickles to the grocery list when the jar is nearly empty. Each gift encountered thrills me beyond measure.

My husband and I like to say that marriage is not a 50/50 proposition; it is perhaps 70/30. Oddly, however, each of us feels as though we are giving the 70 percent. Taking turns in any relationship does not work precisely. If each of us feels we are giving the 70%, why keep bitter accounts of what we are owed? Why not shift our attitude toward giving as pleasure? Shakespeare's Romeo tells Juliet, "The more I give to thee, the more I have." The bottom line is not significant. What matters is that each of us is willing to offer what seems to us the greater share, and each is satisfied (usually!) with the 30% return. We recognize that giving

and getting will fluctuate. Besides, we can always negotiate. Though the immediate balance sheet may not reflect our investments in a relationship, acts of consideration, affection, and support accrue great dividends over time. We pray with Ignatius of Loyola, "Teach us to give and not to count the cost."

Spring days at the nursery, with acres of greenhouse variety, make us want to sample a little of everything in our own gardens. But a hodgepodge of different plant specimens seldom shows well in landscaping. Better a few favorites massed for stunning effect— a wall of jasmine, expanses of peonies, swaths of iris. Profusion creates impact.

Indoors, too many small details register as clutter. Volume, instead, conveys abundance—mounds of dried hydrangea brimming a basket, a great bowl of shells, yards of drapery. Extravagance makes an impression.

Generosity applies to cooking as well. Recipes which require a tablespoon of parsley always amuse me. Really now! What can such a miserly amount of the simple herb do for a dish? Handfuls of herbs are in order—lots of varieties with wild abandon—a bunch of basil, a fist of oregano, tufts of thyme—rich infusions of flavor.

Try one of my favorite herbs, burnet, for a cucumbery complement to fish, salad, fruit, or summer soup. It is not readily available, but is worth seeking out to plant in your own garden.

Time is one commodity in great need of generosity. "Quality time," denoting compressed togetherness, is a delusion. Intimacies develop slowly over extended time together. Speed relationships—child rearing, marriage, or otherwise—do not exist. Ralph Waldo Emerson maintains, "The only gift is a portion of thyself."

One Christmas season, unable to resist a bargain at the farmers' market, my husband purchased an entire crate of pineapples. Before such quantity could perish, we tied each with festive ribbon and made the rounds of friends. Surprisingly, they were charmed by the unexpected fruits on their doorsteps and invited us in. The pineapples, symbols of hospitality, opened doors to spontaneous Christmas spirit.

When it comes to gifts, price need not equate with value. Gifts that cost little or nothing often delight recipients most. Hand-made arts, home-grown bounty, or treats from the kitchen—bread, jam, herbs, salsa, personal specialties— never fail to please. Creativity is always welcome currency.

GIFTS THAT COST

LITTLE OR NOTHING

OFTEN DELIGHT

RECIPIENTS MOST.

I can never repay the sweet generosities extended to me with publication of my books. A friend hosted a book signing in her beautiful home, introducing me to her wide circle of acquaintances, and perfuming the entire house with an extravagant bouquet of fragrant flowers. Another friend surprised and delighted me at a retail book signing by serenading patrons with the glories of her harp. A group of church women who had invited me to speak arranged lush plants, a trellis, fountain, benches, and stepping stones to create an inviting indoor garden. And everywhere I go, people open their hearts and lives to me. I have been particularly touched by the stories that return to me of applications which my modest volumes have found—the realtor who warmed the house of each client with a book at closing, the restaurateur who read meditations at staff meetings, the Hindu woman in India comforted by pages on her deathbed, the Alzheimer's patient who found in prayers the words she had lost, organizations which have placed books at patient bedsides—graces God has blessed. For these and so many other expressions of effusive kindness, I owe a great debt of gratitude.

Grace

Grace connotes refinement, beauty, proportion, courtesy, generosity, and restraint. In our increasingly crass, commercial, and cacophonous world, the term is little used and seldom seems to apply. Although grace may appear to have fallen out of favor, we yearn for it. It generates joy and delight in our outlook, serenity and contentment in our living, respect and harmony in our relationships. As Miguel de Cervantes muses, "Fair and softly goes far."

We need not settle for what is degenerate, depressing, and disturbing. We can, for example, turn off belligerent, mind-numbing television programming, and substitute uplifting, enriching pursuits and stimulating, heartening company.

Grace need not be abandoned because the world around us seems to value it so little. Grace can be revived. Perhaps we cannot change what is coarse, tawdry, and vulgar in the world about us, but we can alter how we experience the world and how the world responds to us by cultivating grace. Being attentive, we can carry grace with us into an often graceless world. I love the prayer of Joan of Arc: "If I am not in God's grace, may God bring me there; if I am in it, may he keep me there." Grace changes everything.

The three graces of Greek mythology were Aglaia (Splendor), Euphrosyne (Mirth), and Thalia (Good Cheer). Their presence imbued gods and mortals with peace and happiness. The gracious person exudes these classic qualities: a splendor of cultivated virtue, beauty, and excellence; a mirthful attitude of lighthearted conviviality; a cheerful demeanor of sincere optimism and hopeful encouragement. Austrian writer Marie Ebner-Eschenbach defines grace as "the outcome of inner harmony."

During my telephone chat with an elderly friend, she remarked, offhandedly, that her maid was polishing her silver. In her 90s, living in a retirement community, she would not likely be entertaining lavishly or formally in the near future, but she was a grand lady of the Old South, who still maintained that one must keep her household in order and her silver polished. After all, she held that even impromptu guests deserve to be pampered and put at ease. And besides, the more often good silver is used and polished, the more beautiful its patina becomes. Her practice applies to keeping our spirits gleaming as well. Anyone with whom we interact deserves our most hospitable selves— polite, indulgent, and attentive. Cultivating courtesy means buffing our grace to a perennial shine.

Grace focuses outward rather than inward. It means giving without thought of return. Grace also means receiving with openness and gratitude. Because it is undeserved, unexpected, and wondrous, grace does not mean trying harder. In fact, the less we try, the more often grace comes to us. Annie Dillard points out, "Beauty and grace are performed whether or not we will or sense them. The least we can do is try to be there."

In a basement box of musty books, I found a yellowing report card from the early 1900s. The teacher's remarks, in a fine, flourishing hand, included a category for comportment. Although the term itself is a little moldy, it needs to be aired and applied. Comportment

GRACE IS A GRATEFUL ATTITUDE THAT EXTENDS BEYOND MEALTIME TO PERMEATE OUR LIVES. extends beyond classroom behavior to conduct appropriate to circumstances. While attending a recent funeral, my husband and I were disturbed by those behind us, talking, joking, and shuffling in their pew, disrespecting the occasion's solemnity. Whether in a classroom, courtroom, doctor's office, library, or restaurant, conventions of behavior are designed to respect a place, its use, and others present.

Jonathan Edwards explains how grace is a life-long pursuit on our heavenward journey: "Grace is but glory begun, and glory is but grace perfected." The essence of grace is elegance, manifested in dress, bearing, speech, and attitude. Such elegance is distinguished by both an outward expression of aesthetic refinement and an inner state of spiritual ease.

William Henry Channing eloquently expresses our aspiration to grace: "To live content with small means; to seek elegance rather than luxury, and refinement rather than fashion; to be worthy, not respectable, and wealthy, not rich; to study hard, think quietly, talk gently, act frankly; to listen to stars and birds, babes and sages, with open heart; to bear all cheerfully, do all bravely, await occasions, hurry never. In a word, to let the spiritual, unbidden and unconscious, grow up through the common—This is to be my symphony."

Gratitude

A busy young mother whom we know dashed to prepare the house for her twin sons' party. Pressed for time, she phoned her husband to pick up a birthday cake on his way home from work. He knew the cake he found would be a hit with the boys—toy cars atop a miniature race track.

He arrived home just before guests arrived. The boys could hardly keep their hands off the enticing cake. Their little fingers curled around the counter's edge, pulling the boys up on tiptoes, the better to see the sweet prize and gleaming cars. After family and friends enjoyed a cook-out, the time had finally come for gifts and cake. The birthday boys danced around their mother's legs, trying their best to be patient as she removed candles from the box and began to insert them in the cake. Icing cracked; the candles would not budge. She thought the cake must be stale; then she saw the Styrofoam. Her husband had brought home the bakery display model.

She could have rebuked him. Instead, she burst into laughter, and now the family has a fun story to tell on Dad. She thanked him for his effort and for helping with the party. Even more significant mistakes can seem less consequential and can be easily diffused if we relinquish our personal idea of perfection, avoid criticism, and respond with appreciation.

"A single grateful thought towards heaven is the most perfect prayer," observes Ephraim Gotthold Lessing. Grace is not simply the rote lines we recite before eating. Grace is a grateful attitude that extends beyond mealtime to permeate our lives. A habit of gratitude means counting the bliss in even the banal. Saying grace is a practice of noting our own small moments of delight, but also of remarking on them, sharing them, and proclaiming the blessing abounding around us. Gratitude multiplies joy for ourselves and others. We want to be quick to recognize and credit those who help and serve

us and to express our pride in those we cherish. Charles Spurgeon counsels us to consecrate our days: "Wash your faith every morning in a bath of praise."

Being a guest requires as much art as being a host. Appreciation begins as soon as an invitation is received. The courtesy of a prompt reply is crucial to the hosts' planning. Arrive bearing gifts: send flowers ahead or bring a small personal gift for both host and hostess—a CD, exquisite cheese, or favorite wine. Keep eyes open and offer any needed help—food preparation, filling glasses, introductions, but do not get in the way. Houseguests should tread lightly in the space of others and let hosts take the lead; adapt to the hosts' schedule by avoiding rising too early or retiring too late; allow hosts private time by reading, taking a walk, or sightseeing alone for a while; reciprocate by taking hosts for lunch, drinks, or dinner or by paying for a tank of gas; never use a host's personal items, such as phone or computer, without asking, and then most judiciously for only true necessity; tidy one's room and bath before departure. And always follow up threshold thanks with a proper note after the occasion. These are the simplest of graces for all the pleasures hosts extend to guests.

I find it easiest to compose a thank-you note immediately after receiving a gift, enjoying a dinner party, being touched by a personal kindness or professional courtesy. While still basking in the pleasure, I find joy in articulating appreciation. And thank-you notes promptly sent double a recipient's delight when the occasion is still fresh in mind. Keeping handsome stationery, pen, and stamps together in a comfortable writing space makes thank-you notes a thoughtful habit.

Regardless of your penmanship, always send a handwritten note. When composing a thank-you, personalize comments and be effusive about your pleasure. Thanks can never include too much praise. Be specific. For a gift, exclaim how perfectly it suits your taste or décor, or describe your plans for the item. For a gift card or cash, express thanks for the giver's generosity. For a dinner party or entertainment, mention a specific dish you loved, the beautiful table, scintillating company, or great time. For a gesture, describe how much it meant to you. When more than a note is required, for a weekend stay or a special kindness, send flowers, wine, or a food specialty; honor with a charity donation; or extend a reciprocal invitation or favor. A thank-you is particularly appreciated when it recognizes the giver's special efforts to please.

W. H. Auden counsels, "Let all your thinks be thanks." Yet it is not always easy to be thankful, especially if we are assaulted by disappointment, illness, tragedy, or loss. If we make gratitude a practice, however, we will more readily find blessing in adversity. When we recognize that all of life is a gift, we can learn to accept that whatever befalls us sanctifies our lives. An anonymous adage reminds us, "When you have thanked your God for every blessing sent, what time will there remain for murmurs and lament?"

In the hospital following his stroke, my father could barely speak or move. He required help even to sip water or to shift a pillow. Until he began to recover his abilities, all his needs were tended by someone else. Yet, despite his debilities, he always managed the considerable effort to say, "Thank you," for the smallest kindnesses of his nurses, family, and wife. Even when he was capable of so little, his whispered gratitude encouraged his caregivers. For my father, gratitude was his way of life, and a benediction for others. He shared the attitude of Alphonse Karr: "Some people are always grumbling because roses have thorns. I am thankful that thorns have roses."

Our back yard garden is too shady for vegetables now that trees have matured, so we have transformed the site into a friendship and memorial garden with namesake plants. In it reside Miss Pinkie, a cheerful coral camellia given to me by a spirited red-haired friend; HydranJoe, a hot pink hydrangea from a red-bearded friend with a green thumb; another quirky-growing camellia for a friend who always heard his own drummer; stately grape-scented iris, a favorite from my mother's garden; auburn mums and a concrete resemblance of our red-furred feline friend buried there. The formerly wasted space is becoming a place to recollect the gifts with which our dear ones, lost and living, bless our lives in their distinctive ways. Jean Baptiste Massieu depicts gratitude as "the memory of the heart."

Growth

My husband calls my decorating style "early flea market," which is an appropriate tag. Much of our home is furnished from Saturday morning forays to European flea markets, where I might spy a treasure, haggle for a bargain, and snag a prize, recounting the morning's exploits to my husband over a lunch of steaming soup and local wine at a nearby bistro he had discovered. En route home in the back of a streetcar, we may wedge a wicker table, tote a picture frame, or balance a chandelier. As our tastes evolved and budget allowed, we pared furnishings that no longer reflected our affinities and replaced them with new discoveries. Our home has become an expression of our continually growing selves.

Wearing a hair style that has outgrown its life expectancy? Spending too much time on a do that never seems to do well? Perhaps a short, chic cut is in order, an off-the-face style, a wisp of bangs, or a soft color. Why not dispense with fuss, brighten makeup, and gain easy elegance? Upgrading image instills confidence and makes us feel comfortable in our own skin. Change for its own sake is not necessarily better if made simply to follow a trend or to induce a rush. But change can elicit improvement when designed to enhance the changing complexion of our lives.

A decorating change can seem such a simple switch. We move a picture on a wall and notice the nearby table is now out of proportion, so we exchange the table for another, which means chairs must shift, but the divan then needs moving, and lamps have to find new locations. Before we can say, "Honey, can you help?" the entire room requires rearranging.

Life demands similar readjustments, and they often seem ongoing. Just when we think we have settled into a comfortable stasis, the vicissitudes of living insist we adjust and adapt. A lithe spirit will make us more flexible in accommodating the inevitable shuffle imposed by change. We would do well to emulate the attitude of Sara Teasdale: "I make the most of all that comes and the least of all that goes."

When my mother and we young sisters visited our great Aunt Emma in a retirement home near our house, residents would often ask the question familiar to children, "What do you want to be when you grow up?" Spurred by the writing opportunities my creative teacher provided, I would answer, "An author." Yet I did not begin my own writing career, despite teaching college composition for decades, until I was nearly 50. I needed time to cultivate the experiences and insights from which my writing would draw. Developing any talent requires the burnishing of time.

Eric Milner-White prays to avoid the close-mindedness of self-satisfaction: "Suffer me never to think that I have knowledge enough to need no teaching, wisdom enough to need no correction, talents enough to need no grace, goodness enough to need no progress, humility enough to need no repentance, devotion enough to need no quickening, strength sufficient without thy Spirit, lest, standing still, I fall back for evermore."

Change is often fearful and uncomfortable. It requires us to assume challenges that strain our capabilities. But in order to grow, we must abandon our clutch on the comfortable, relinquish our yearning for certainty, focus on hope, and aim for unfamiliar horizons. Only by freshening our most tenacious personal clichés, can we allow the insecurity and vulnerability needed to grow. The Apostle Paul's example heartens us: "But one thing I do: Forgetting what is behind and straining toward what is ahead, I press on toward the goal to win the prize for which God has called me heavenward in Christ Jesus" (Philippians 313b-14).

In the garden, organic matter from the previous season feeds new growth. If we are to be fully alive, everyday must have a little death in it. Releasing what is negative, past, and spent is necessary for renewal. The humus of our lives is enriched by the compost of our past experiences.

On the ice skating rink, the ball field, and the dance floor, physical grace has always eluded me. Yet despite my lack of training or skill in any of these arts, I have always imagined the thrill of skimming across a pond, catching the fly ball, or floating with a partner to music. I may still have hope. Author Pearl Buck long aspired to dance as she remembered her mother doing with such grace. Yet only as a dowager did she begin lessons, discovering late in life the delights of dance. She held the opinion that "growth itself contains the germ of happiness."

When we are young, the years seem long because they are filled with new and memorable experiences. As we age, little is new to us; years seem to fly as days are compressed in sameness. Filling our days with stimulating experiences will make our years feel long and full again. Edith Wharton articulates the importance of growth: "In spite of illness, in spite even of archenemy sorrow, one can remain alive long past the usual date of disintegration if one is unafraid of change, insatiable in curiosity, interested in big things, and happy in small ways."

The key to growth is meaningful and fulfilling change, encouraging the best in us. What goals can we set for ourselves by trying a new activity—an opera, rollerblading; improving health—more exercise, a healthful diet; fostering a relationship—making a new friend, mending family ties; expanding professional enrichment; lending a volunteer hand; changing a habit; learning a new skill; replacing complaint with action? Identifying specific ways we can grow will move us from inertia to action. "We know what we are," writes William Shakespeare, "but know not what we may be."

"*WE* KNOW WHAT WE ARE, BUT KNOW NOT WHAT WE MAY BE."

Harmony

G ood cooks know how to harmonize ingredients for just the right taste. They adjust acid, sweetness, or salt to improve balance in a dish. They select wines to complement or emphasize flavors. They coordinate courses to liven the palate. Cooking is a practiced art of synthesizing taste in pleasing combination.

Aesthetics matter, too. Family and guests appreciate a beautiful table, harmonizing dinnerware and linens. I like to set a bird-egg blue breakfast cloth with brown stoneware, feather-patterned bread plates, and bird nest napkins given to me by a friend. As a centerpiece, I may fill a small birdbath with straw, a cement bird from the garden, and marble eggs. The avian theme sings of spring.

Matched table settings can feel predictable. When mixing compatible items for seasonal displays, quirky often trumps coordinated. I have decorated a buffet table with candlesticks, deer antlers, and gilded grapes, entwined with strands of pearl and gold beads, reflecting holiday opulence. On the casual flip side, we have hosted an outdoor Low-Country boil using paper bags as placemats over simple gingham tablecloths with bright umbrellas overhead. Contents tucked away in cupboards and closets may spur your own inventive compositions.

A house in which every room is a different color and style can feel disconnected and jarring. Linking a decorating theme, using the same flooring, repeating a fabric, or carrying a wall color from room to room creates a harmonic whole. A calming sense of coherence results. Felix Mendelssohn submits, "The essence of the beautiful is unity in variety."

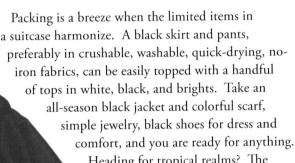

Packing is a breeze when the limited items in
a suitcase harmonize. A black skirt and pants,
preferably in crushable, washable, quick-drying, no-
iron fabrics, can be easily topped with a handful
of tops in white, black, and brights. Take an
all-season black jacket and colorful scarf,
simple jewelry, black shoes for dress and
comfort, and you are ready for anything.
Heading for tropical realms? The
same equation works in warm-
weather whites or
natural linen.

In the grocery store recently, I
watched a long-legged daddy with
a curly-haired toddler in hand. For
each stride of his long blue jeans, the
little pink leggings did an unsteady
three-step. Her daddy kept a brisk pace, seemingly
oblivious to the demanding scamper of his tiny charge. How often
are we out of step even with those to whom we are attached? In a
hurry, we forget the needs of others. Improving our awareness will
help us to step in stride. Ralph Waldo Emerson relates the benefits
of harmony: "There is no beautifier of complexion, or form, or
behavior, like the wish to scatter joy and not pain around us."

Relinquishing an injustice, ill will, or irritation is terribly hard, but
like an overloaded purse, a grudge can be heavy to carry. Relieving
the weight requires clearing out that messy tube of resentment, those
shredded tissues of disappointment, the compact full of anger, and
dropping all that messy debris we have been hauling around into
God's hands. He can help us to forgive and open our hearts to the
blessings of a relationship.

We encounter plenty of occasions, too, when we need forgiveness for our own blunders and oversights. "I'm sorry, BUT . . ." dilutes our sincerity. When we are at fault, it is important to recognize our failing, accept responsibility, apologize sincerely and specifically to those we have hurt, and change our behavior.

Most of us, however, have trouble apologizing. My husband and I have discovered that the habit of praying together before meals makes it somewhat easier to convey our apologies while speaking to God together. We can be more comfortable saying to God, "I am sorry I was so thoughtless, irritable, or preoccupied. Please help me to let my husband know how much I love and appreciate him." Praying in my husband's presence lets him know I recognize my offense, am genuinely sorry for it, and intend to change my behavior, but somehow this prayed confession is often more manageable than admitting to him, "Boy, did I make a mistake!" Plus, God can heal the relationship.

"Let us forgive each other," proposes Leo Tolstoy, "—only then will we live in peace." Harmony is a deep sense of communion with ourselves, with our earth, with each other, and with our God, who can synchronize all things, in a most incoherent world, to work together for good. ✒

Imagination

"The imagination needs time to browse," claims Thomas Merton. Imagination is often a matter of putting the familiar to new uses. Early in her career, designer Coco Chanel translated utilitarian blazer wool and underwear jersey into ingenious casual sportswear. The color of mourning became her all-occasion "little black dress." She layered ropes of pearls and beads over simple belted sweaters. Later, she designed nubby, boxy suits as a departure from voluminous ankle-length skirts and nipped waists of Dior-inspired fashions. Her revolutionary looks have become today's classics.

Jewelry can be especially fun when worn in unexpected ways—a vintage brooch pinned on a purse, at the belt, or on the cuff of a blouse; earrings serving as cufflinks; long beads knotted as a belt; a stretch bracelet twisted as a hair tie; a necklace worn as a bracelet. I enjoy pinning a small silver bee at the wrist of a sweater to inspire industry. In an unlikely place, a favorite piece can capture attention, convey personal significance, or recall a happy memory.

Imagination makes for great company. When we want our spirits lifted, or need a great guest for a party, which friend do we phone? . . . Likely the one with wit and snap, who thinks for herself, someone exhilarating and slightly cheeky. Concern about what people will think or how we will be perceived can suffocate originality. Nothing is more boring than uniformity. If we would like to be that friend whom others call, we might aim to be less predictable. Imagination and wonder can even make us look and feel better. "The best cosmetic in the world," says Mary Meek Atkeson, "is an active mind that is always finding something new."

And, of course, originality, ingenuity, and resourcefulness are qualities prized by employers in all professions. "Logic will get you from A to B," concludes Albert Einstein. "Imagination will take you everywhere." Flights of fancy cost nothing, but they may be the best ticket you can buy to thrilling and rewarding destinations. Go on— see how far dreams can take you. 🙰

Imitation

A suntan was once considered a sign of the servant class, which labored outdoors. Women of earlier centuries whitened their faces with poisonous paint and chalk and carried parasols to preserve pale skin in efforts to resemble the leisure class. Only in the twentieth century did bronzed skin become fashionable when wealthy and fashionable Europeans returned glowing from sunny holidays in southern climes, and women's lifestyles turned to outdoor sport and activity. With today's concerns about sun damage, pale skin is looking good again.

Skin care is requisite to putting a woman's best face forward—gentle cleansing, regular moisturizing, faithful sunscreen, and subtle make-up. But skin vogue is often adopted wholesale without considering consequences beyond the superficial. Because the effects of some of today's skin care chemicals and treatments remain unknown, researching claims, health ramifications, and alternatives to popular cosmetics and procedures can help us make prudent decisions about their use. We are all eager to maintain our appearance, to look as wonderful as celebrities and friends going to lengths for looks. Imitation has always been the lifeblood of fashion, but it needs to be applied with informed personal judgment.

I am always flattered when I find one of my own decorative ideas introduced into the home, garden, or wardrobe of a friend—faux animal hide upholstery, the massing of caladiums, a belted white shirt with a single piece of bold jewelry. And I keep my own eyes open to borrow styles from other inventive sources. Inspiration from fashion and decorating magazines can be adapted to a modest budget with knock-off fabrics or department store accessories. Even designers borrow from each other. Benjamin Franklin admits, "Originality is the art of concealing your sources." Much of the fun of shopping is bagging ideas—the combination of natural textures in a floral arrangement, fresh colors to introduce into a wardrobe, a novel design for valances. I count an excursion success when I can bring home creative looks to fashion in my own style.

Whom do we admire? We can become our better selves by emulating the best. We need not choose as our role models those most handy, if family or friends are not so admirable; nor must we follow the most ubiquitous examples, as television's lowest common denominators. It is useful to contemplate whose qualities we desire to claim as our own, and to set about reflecting them. Hohn Weiss states, "Imitation forms our manners, our opinions, our very lives."

It IS USEFUL TO CONTEMPLATE WHOSE QUALITIES WE DESIRE TO CLAIM AS OUR OWN, AND TO SET ABOUT REFLECTING THEM.

I have had the great gift of wonderful parents to emulate. Although my parents' virtues serve as my dominant influence, I also credit my Aunt Irene for her own inspiring refinements. A working mother, she always dressed tastefully with coordinating high heels and bracelets. In her modest home, decorated with antiques, she created a quiet oasis. The ticking of her mantle clock kept a gentle tempo; even its bells knew to whisper when they chimed. A gracious hostess, she set a beautiful buffet with her collection of crystal and linens. And she single-handedly kept Hallmark in business, sending cards and personal notes to all her extended family for every holiday, birthday, or memorable occasion. Each night she eased to sleep with a book. Because she entertained only lovely thoughts, she could look forward to beautiful dreams. Like my mother's, her disposition was ever tranquil. Both women were model ladies for a young girl who was just learning to become a lady herself.

When I drive past the character word of the week on the neighborhood elementary school signboard, I respond ambiguously. I am pleased to see character being encouraged, but I wonder whether parents may be abdicating the teaching of virtues along with other vital parental responsibilities. Whose values do we hope to instill in our children? Which virtues do we prize? Are we doing our part in modeling and emphasizing them? Why not orient our children and ourselves to the divine and perfect source of all goodness? St Paul admonishes, "Be imitators of God, therefore, as dearly loved children and live a life of love, just as Christ loved us and gave himself up for us as a fragrant offering and sacrifice to God" (Ephesians 5:1-2).

Imperfection

Every night we sleep under a blanket of ivy, lovingly appliquéd and embroidered in a trellis pattern by my mother. In one corner of the quilt, tiny stitches emboss a spider web design. This emblem from nature is characteristic of traditional quilts. Incorporated in an otherwise regular pattern of even handiwork, the spider web is a symbolic reminder that nothing is perfect under God's heaven.

I have furnished much of our home by reclaiming cast-offs and undesirables, giving them opportunity to shine—the slim chest with beautiful Italian lines, stripped of garish yellow paint; junk-shop lamps found in piles of pieces, reassembled and revived with new shades; a filthy French chair shredded by barn cats, refinished and upholstered in brocade; a damaged needlework, cut to pillow-size. What appears on the surface to be junk is easy to ignore, and, of course, selecting beautiful objects from a home furnishing store is simpler. But with an eye for potential and a penchant for the unique, the fun is discovering an overlooked piece to transform into a personal work of art. Sam Levenson reminds us that people need salvaging, too. "People even more than things have to be restored, renewed, revived, reclaimed, and redeemed and redeemed and redeemed. Never throw out anybody."

Claw tracks mar a chest where our cat has taken fright, a permanent dip sags in a cushion, and upholstery roses have faded to blush. The ruined finish of a drop leaf table, near an open window in an unexpected shower, is concealed with a square of velvet-embossed yardage hemmed as a tablecloth. Our rooms are truly living rooms, scarred and aged by the tumble of years. We no longer see the flaws, however, only the memories and comforts that constitute home.

In fact, we feel a certain easy pleasure in our worn and cherished furnishings. Already blemished, they do not require cautious handling

as do perfect rooms that are rarely used. Yellowed silk disintegrates and slips from a lamp shade, insouciant in its state of dishabille. Our familiar spaces grow relaxed, like the company of intimate relationships. John Ruskin points out why blemishes are so valuable to the human condition: "All things are literally better, lovelier, and more beloved for the imperfections which have been divinely appointed, that the law of human life may be Effort, and the law of human judgment Mercy."

A PERFECT LOOK IS DIFFICULT, IF NOT IMPOSSIBLE, TO ACHIEVE. A perfect look is difficult, if not impossible, to achieve. We all have to contend with budgetary constraints, family requirements, awkward room shapes, existing landscapes, or an irregular figure. But finding workable solutions can be a matter of simply identifying what to downplay and what to emphasize.

Does your kitchen window offer an unsightly view of the neighbor's cluttered garage? Plant a trellis and cover it with vines. Has a wool coat been chewed by hungry summer moths? Conceal nibbles with a large eye-catching shawl. Do you have more Thanksgiving guests than dinnerware? Intersperse your best with alternate settings of dollar-store dishes. Improvised improvements may even inject an unexpected flair. Amos Bronson Alcott assures us that "we mount to heaven mostly on the ruins of our cherished schemes, finding our failures were successes."

Insisting on perfection can actually harm our selves and our relationships with others. Perfectionists may be less open to exploring new directions, focused instead on the prescribed and

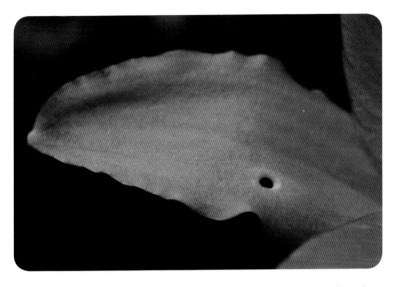

predictable. They may be more easily depressed, too, when the job, marriage, figure, or house does not achieve an inaccessible standard.

Perfectionists may also be more judgmental and demanding of others, whom they expect to conform to unrealistic ideals. To better respond to the perceived deficiencies of those around us, we might recognize that as human "beings," we are all incomplete, ever in the act of becoming and equally valued by God.

Individuality

My father could never remember the names of his three daughters' little girlfriends who came to play with Barbie dolls or celebrate birthdays, or sleep over, or stage backyard performances, or giggle about nothing, so he addressed each of them as Mary. Oddly, they always responded to this name, though it was not their own. Because our girlfriends enjoyed my father's pleasant nature, not one of them corrected him. While I recall this memory with amusement, it does cause me to consider the many Marys in the world today, happy to answer to someone else's identity, who may

EXAMINING OURSELVES

WITH A CRITICAL EYE

OR SEEKING THE ADVICE

OF AN OBJECTIVE

PROFESSIONAL WILL

HELP TO DETERMINE

LOOKS WHICH ARE

MOST FLATTERING.

benefit from the words of Epictetus: "Know who you are; and then adorn yourself accordingly."

When Jacqueline Kennedy Onassis redecorated her New York home, she merely freshened rooms with fabrics resembling those she replaced. She maintained a version of her same hair style through much of her adulthood. Katherine Hepburn kept her upswept hairdo as well, using the same homemade rolled-up newspaper curlers from her starlet days her entire life. She wore trademark trousers and turtleneck sweaters for decades. Through the years, style icon Audrey Hepburn chose variations of the classic black sheath. Astonishingly, she also kept her figure. Her fashion designer and friend Hubert de Givenchy never had to modify the mannequin he made for her original fitting in 1954. These women had a sure sense of their own style and adhered to what suited them best. Rabbi Ben Azai uses a garden metaphor: "Women, like roses, should wear only their own colors, and emit no borrowed perfumes."

Advertising's ubiquitous enticements are designed to seduce us into wanting the newest and most current. But the majority of today's "must-haves" will not be right for us. Youth may be a time to try trendy fashions and to explore variety, but ultimately, we will want to identify our own personal style. Examining ourselves with a critical eye or seeking the advice of an objective professional will help to determine looks which are most flattering.

Editing refines our tastes. If we do not look our best in an outfit, we can donate, consign, or recycle it. Rather than crowd a closet with misfits, culling contents to only clothes we love wearing will express ourselves to our self-assured advantage. And think of the time saved when everything in our closet suits us well.

A wardrobe should not be changeless and boring, however. We want clothes to reflect our personal affinities and affections—quirky is okay, even a dash of eccentricity for spice. A lawyer friend defies all guesses about her profession in sweeping circular skirts and jeweled sweaters. She is confident enough to express her own custom style. Once we find our personal vision and express it with flair, we are no longer slaves to the fickle fads of fashion. Benjamin Disraeli remarks, "The originality of a subject is in its treatment." Rules of taste need not be rigid. By trusting instincts, we can design our own distinctive allure. After all, we are defined by our enthusiasms.

Landscaping for home builders seldom resembles landscaping for home owners. Construction companies seek curb appeal, while homeowners seek life-enhancing plants. This clash of interests became apparent when we moved into our current home. Near the street, crepe myrtles marched in rows like soldiers presenting colors, but behind, a naked bed lay exposed to view from our front windows. Stark wood fences divided too-close neighbors on a narrow lot. Sprawling evergreens swamped a small kitchen plot near the back door. And scent was ignored altogether. My husband and I set to work, planting gardenias in front, whose glossy green we could enjoy year round from inside as well as out. We covered ugly fencing with jasmine, evergreen with bonus spring scent, and installed cypress along lot lines for noise insulation. A profusion of herbs transformed our kitchen garden. Now the landscape accommodates our own tastes and enriches the way we live.

What is the appeal of so much vicarious pleasure—spectator sports, television, gossip, celebrity? What is the fascination and entertainment in what everyone else is doing? Instead of watching, listening to, and ruminating about the exploits of others, why not invest as much time and energy in investigating our own interests, developing our own talents, cultivating our own experiences, and creating our own stories? Even less than proficient efforts can make a contribution. As Henry van Dyke points out, "Use what talents you possess; the woods would be very silent if no birds sang except those that sang best."

On occasions when I have read a book after seeing the movie which it inspired, I am always disappointed. I no longer have the pleasure of imagining characters and scenes in my own mind's eye because the film's images override the mental pictures I may have envisioned myself. I want my own life to be the book I write, not an adapted version of someone else's conceit.

Embracing our own distinctive natures can be challenging. We often go to great lengths to seek approval, to be liked. But Marcus Aurelius invites us to consider, "Does what is praised become better?" When we learn to enjoy our own company, to value our own opinions, we are not desperate for relationships that do not function well, which may even diminish or damage us. Once we can find satisfaction inherent in our own choices without requiring affirmation from others, we are on our way to becoming our original, variegated selves.

GAINING CONFIDENCE IN OUR DECISIONS REQUIRES LEARNING TO IDENTIFY THE CRITERIA BY WHICH WE JUDGE.

When traveling, we are disappointed to find increasing homogeneity. Formerly idiosyncratic cities with their own identifiable characters are becoming, in many respects, difficult to distinguish from one another. The same shops and restaurants can be found from one coast of our country to another, and even around the globe. And what is perhaps more surprising, travelers patronize these comfortably familiar institutions instead of seeking what makes a locale uncommon—the idiosyncratic pleasures for which we leave home. Cities, as well as personal tastes, can easily lose their uniqueness to uniformity. Our souls, too, can be abandoned when we buy into standards of the world instead of heeding our incomparable God, whose "way is perfect" (2 Samuel 22:31a).

Gaining confidence in our decisions requires learning to identify the criteria by which we judge. Those standards become reasoned and well informed through reading, travel, observation, study, and experience. When it comes to determining spiritual principles, we can avoid bending to the unreliable breezes of self-gratification or circumstance by acknowledging God's own immutable truths.

Joy

What colors make you happy? Do sunny yellow and volts of red make you feel energized or over-charged? Do misty blue and grassy green calm you or put you to sleep? By identifying how colors make you feel, you can inject an appropriate palette into your rooms and wardrobe. Keep in mind that your color choice may vary from a room where you rest to one where you work, or from a blouse for business to one for weekends, but the hues should make you feel positive. Color can be a quick, dependable infusion of cheer.

I love the story of Jesus making pancakes for his disciples. Well, okay, it was not pancakes exactly; it was actually a breakfast of bread and fish. But here he was, giving his friends a savory start to the day (John 21). When, as children, my brother, sisters, and I occasionally stayed overnight with my favorite Aunt Ruth, she would make us pancakes in the shape of little bears—two small blobs of batter for the body, two smaller drops of batter for ears, served with a slather of butter and drizzle of syrup. Simply sweet, simply delightful. Breakfast—what a gift to others or to ourselves. It is worth rising a few minutes early to savor a peaceful interlude as we ease into the day.

"The cheerful heart has a continual feast," relates Proverbs 15:15b. Joy is not the practice of coping with the bad, but rather of noticing the good—a flamingo sunrise, laughter with a friend, whipped cream, freedom from pain, fresh sheets, a clear mind, summer flip-flops. Bliss surrounds us. Across the street, a builder in his tool-belt pirouettes on a beam, a felicitous ballet; outside the window, a golden orb-weaver spider builds a web in dewy shrubs; inside the garage, a family of wrens nests in garden gloves. To

"THE CHEERFUL HEART HAS A CONTINUAL FEAST."

claim such enchantments requires only the custom of open eyes. Henry Ward Beecher cautions that blessings before us easily escape if we are inattentive: "There are joys which long to be ours. God sends ten thousand truths, which come to us like birds seeking inlet; but we are shut up to them, and so they bring us nothing, but sit and sing awhile upon the roof, and then fly away."

Happiness is an emotion dependent on circumstances, but joy is a state which comes from knowing our spiritual destiny. C. S. Lewis defines joy as "the serious business of heaven." When we believe God's promises, joy becomes a habit. An older friend finds the good in a day when she can get out of a chair with only one push, or when she can glory in a great gold moon and smell jasmine perfuming her yard. Her joy is not diminished with age and infirmity, but enhanced by the assurance of her faith. "Some days there won't be a song in your heart," sympathizes Emory Austin. "Sing anyway."

Regularly I saw my mother plant, pot, water, feed, weed, dig, trim, tote, mulch, hoe, and prune. But I often wondered why I seldom saw my mother simply sit down to enjoy her extensive and beloved flower garden. I came to realize, however, that her joy was the gardening itself. She is right about delight. Fun is in the doing, the learning, the quest, the work. She and Ralph Waldo Emerson have the right attitude: "The reward of a thing well done is to have done it."

FUN IS IN THE DOING, THE LEARNING, THE QUEST, THE WORK.

In her brown uniform, the delivery woman bounds up the steps, raps quickly on the door, shares a big smile and a brief chat, then bounces back to her truck. Even when our mood is down, we cannot help but feel better that this lady is part of our day. Her blithe spirit buoys us and returns to boost her own spirit. One of my favorite adages is aromatic: "Happiness is a perfume you cannot pour on others without getting a few drops on yourself." To whose addresses are we delivering parcels of cheer?

We can wish away life in hoping for a better job, a more perfect husband, a stronger body, more stimulating friends, a larger bank account, greater success. Notice how wishes are expressed in comparative form. Often our desires are increased versions of what we now possess. Rather than yearn for the greater and better, why not focus on the greatness and good of gifts already ours?—a husband's encircling arms, strength for the day, dependable friends, satisfactions of work. Here are our joys, generous and near.

Johann Wolfgang von Goethe enumerates the "nine requisites for contented living: health enough to make work a pleasure; wealth enough to support your needs; strength enough to battle difficulties and overcome them; grace enough to confess your sins and forsake them; patience enough to toil until some good is accomplished; charity enough to see some good in your neighbor; love enough to move you to be useful and helpful to others; faith enough to make real the things of God; hope enough to remove all anxious fears concerning the future."

$\mathcal{E}$ARLY IRIDESCENCE SHIMMERS

AND RIMS THE AMETHYST CLOUDS

WITH THE FRESH PERSPECTIVE

OF A LUMINOUS NEW DAY.

Light

When planning a decorating project, remember to observe how the light changes in a room with the seasons and time of day. A pale yellow, perfect in soft morning light, may appear bleached by afternoon, or too chipper for evening. In other exposures, the shade may cheer the dawn and glow gold at dark. Light will also affect the coordinating of carpet, upholstery, and accessories. Remember, too, that textures absorb light while glossy surfaces reflect. Watch the quality of light spilling through windows, and notice its effect to guide your choices.

Mirrors can enhance and disperse light in a dark room. Hung opposite windows, they introduce even greater illumination. An image of a busy street or industrial building can be unwelcome in a living space, however. Careful of the views we entertain, we want to be conscious of what we reflect. Edith Wharton elucidates: "There are two ways of spreading light: to be the candle or the mirror that receives it."

Nature loves a shimmer. Snail tracings glint with moonlight, dew glistens at dawn, icicles cast frosty prisms, and iridescent feathers shift hues in the sun. Why not bring radiance into the dining room? Polished wood, burnished silver, metallic threads in linen, gleaming plates, and translucent crystal illuminate a table. Lit with candles, the setting twinkles; guests glow with warmth and welcome.

As for apparel, one of the most flattering garments a woman can wear is a well-tailored white shirt. Beneath a dark blazer, under a pull-over or cardigan, or on its own, white reflects light to brighten the countenance. Crisp and fit, the classic creates an instant face lift.

Pearls have been prized throughout history for their luster, both their surface refraction of light and their inner glow. The iridescence of pearls is fashioned by irritants. When a piece of foreign matter, like coral, shell, or bone, cannot be expelled, the oyster or mussel coats it with layers of nacre, its shell-building material. To create cultured pearls, the shell is opened, and an irritant is inserted. Over time, layers of nacre build a pearl's classic, cherished sheen.

The brilliant fire of gemstones—emeralds, diamonds, rubies—is designed when molten rock, called magma, seeps into cavities of the earth's shifting mantle. At that point, high temperatures and pressure are exerted. When the fluid moves through earth's crust, above the mantle, magma cools and crystallizes. Over centuries, gems are formed. The sparkle of our own lives is created by perseverance in adversity. Irritants, pressures, and hardships become, over time, the prized jewels which brighten our character.

Have you ever seen sundogs? Sundogs are bright arches around the sun in a winter sky. On a chill and hazy day, their parenthetical expression reminds me that the grey today is only a digression, a brief interval in a brighter continuity.

Sunrises and sunsets of the Midwest Plains can be breathtaking—shocking fuchsia, brilliant copper, stunning purple linger at the horizon and transform the landscape into jeweled vistas. In our home in the South, we have no western view to catch our sunsets, and sunrises are visible only from our small kitchen window, often obscured by trees. But what delight when I can glimpse the morning sun's pastel arrival. Early iridescence shimmers and rims the amethyst clouds with the fresh perspective of a luminous new day. Daily redemption materializes in our emergence from dark into light. Emily Dickinson captures the attitude of expectancy: "Not knowing when the dawn will come / I open every door."

Movement

A room's dancing fire, breezy fan, billowing curtains; a garden's tumbling water, stirring chimes, flitting bees; a wardrobe's glint of gold, sweep of a satin, patent sheen—movement activates our senses and inspires interest.

Budgeting for a family with four youngsters, Mother seldom splurged on clothes for herself. Perhaps this is why I remember a rare trip to a local department store, where the elevator operator whisked us, breathless, to ladies' wear for a special Christmas purchase. I can still recall Mother selecting a stunning bronze taffeta dress with full circle skirt. I adored the way her dress' iridescent colors shifted in the light, the swishing sound as she walked or crossed her legs in shimmery nylon stockings. Mother must have sensed my admiration, for when the style slipped from fashion, she altered that dazzling dress into a swirling skirt for me. I wonder if she knows how many lustrous delights she has passed along to me.

My favorite old furniture pieces were often reincarnated for versatile service as we changed quarters during my husband's military career. Living room lamps shifted to the study. A dining room chest moved to the bedroom. Chairs migrated wherever they comfortably fit. Antique pieces are particularly valuable, not only for their workmanship and detail, but for their chameleon quality. When their original use is a mystery, we feel free to adapt them creatively to our own uses.

Although we tend to use rooms for distinct and separate purposes, we can enhance their versatility by adapting their function. A dining room may be lined in stately bookcases, the dining table serving as a library reference table between meals. A study may double as a guest bedroom with desk space behind louvered doors and a pull-out divan in lush upholstery.

Progressive spaces in the course of an evening's entertaining can also be fun. Drinks might be served on a sun porch or terrace, dinner in the dining room, and coffee in the living room. Moving venues changes scenery, encourages guests to mingle, and freshens conversation. The evening becomes a truly moveable feast from foyer welcomes to lamp-lit goodbyes on the porch.

Consider the pleasure home offers when we return from a trip. Favorite objects feel fresh. Our recharged perspective revives delight in familiar surroundings. As simple alternatives to going away, we might shuffle tablescapes, swap artwork, roll up seasonal rugs, or store items for a time to renew appreciation of acquisitions we love and to inject life into a room. A holiday from the ordinary gives movement to routine. When we take a different route to work, try an uncharacteristic fashion, chat with someone new, we may view the world and ourselves differently. Imagine the unexpected excursions when we are open to change, to new ideas, to anchovies on our pizza.

WHEN WE CAN SLACKEN DEMANDS OF OURSELVES AND OTHERS, RECOGNIZE NOT EVERY CHOICE IS CRITICAL, FORGIVE AND LEARN FROM ERROR, WE DEVELOP RESILIENCE.

You are having scintillating conversation with fascinating people when a visit to the powder room reveals lipstick on your teeth. Don't you wish that someone would have discreetly informed you instead of trying so hard to avoid the obvious? Why are we less willing to hear constructive criticism of our personal faults and flaws? Why deny, defend, and excuse, when gratitude may be in order? We can feel challenged moving from well-worn ruts, from our comfortable, if inaccurate, conceptions of our selves. But we may no longer recognize our own deficiencies. The concern and assistance of someone who cares can impel us toward improvement. "Learning," says Jiddu Krishnamurti, "is movement from moment to moment."

An airline stewardess, taking drink orders, stopped at the row of a father traveling with his young daughter. "And what would you like, Miss?" she leaned to asked.

"I'll have a chocolate shake," the child responded.

The stewardess smiled, and without missing a beat, replied, "I'll give you a shake," taking the young girl gently by her slim shoulders and giving her a playful wiggle.

Sometimes, like this little girl, we are confident about what we want from life, but often we get a gentle, or not so gentle, shake-up instead. Life is seldom static, ever in flux. When what we wanted or thought we deserved is not possible, flexibility is required. We must readjust our expectations, shrug our shoulders, and select from a limited menu.

When we can slacken demands of ourselves and others, recognize not every choice is critical, forgive and learn from error, we develop resilience. Just as stretching loosens joints, limbs, and spine to make one's frame more comfortable and capable, a supple spirit can adjust, adapt, and let go.

Accustomed to the open plains of western Kansas, where gales seldom rest, my college roommate loved gusty days when wind whipped jackets and tangled hair. Blowing weather made her feel alive and animated. While we are rarely comfortable buffeted by the currents of change, those blustery assaults can energize and impel us to alter course or to lean into challenges with increased resourcefulness, to tie back our hair and sail for all we are worth.

Nature

I love to bring outdoor elements indoors with natural objects, colors, and patterns. Shells capture the sea; plants breathe a garden breath; birds' nests perch on door frames; tortoise shells bask on tabletops; lilies lean from rugs and sconces; birds nestle in a needlepoint bower; shams and sheers bloom with roses; peacocks parade on a pillow; sylvan glazes splash majolica; chairs prance on deer feet; and artwork invites us into parks, streams, and groves. Colors from outdoors offer infinite inspiration—the bright magenta of beets, happy gold of tarragon blossoms, glade greens, autumn amber, brown of a wren wing, a rinse of blue water, or dusting of pale sand. Decorating borrowed from nature blurs the boundary between exterior and interior. Nature's incomparable inspiration is described in Luke 12:27: "Consider how the lilies grow. They do not labor or spin. Yet I tell you, not even Solomon in all his splendor was dressed like one of these."

Feeling dull, depleted, distressed, depressed? Nothing will banish the blahs more quickly than a walk outdoors. I promise. After even a short stroll, a breath of fresh air, and a glimpse of

creation, one cannot possibly return indoors without a boost to the spirit. An acquaintance with nature animates the whole family.

We enroll children in sports, music lessons, computer classes—every conceivable extra-curricular activity. Yet often we fail to introduce children to one of the greatest enrichments in which we could engage them—an appreciation of nature. This pursuit does not involve enrollment fees, long commutes, or competitions. The natural world is as close as a backyard or neighborhood park.

With a little encouragement, children will be fascinated by great gifts just outside the door. Join youngsters in exploring nature, using all the senses. Float leaves and petals in a birdbath or puddle, listen for distinct bird calls, taste wild onion grass, feel a ladybug creep along an arm, touch bark and moss, splash in water gushing from a downspout, or laze in a grassy tickle and imagine shapes in drifting clouds. Take a nature walk with a disposable camera. Snap shots of the child, and let the child photograph discoveries. As with any unfamiliar exposure, children need a little nudge to open their eyes to new mysteries and delights. As questions arise, help them find answers in books or computer searches. Or simply shoo children outdoors, and let them make their own discovery, as Aristotle did, that "in all things of nature there is something of the marvelous."

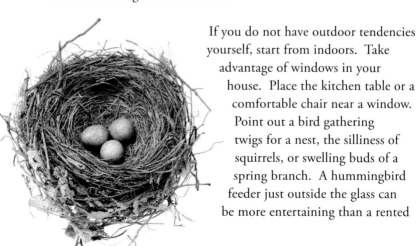

If you do not have outdoor tendencies yourself, start from indoors. Take advantage of windows in your house. Place the kitchen table or a comfortable chair near a window. Point out a bird gathering twigs for a nest, the silliness of squirrels, or swelling buds of a spring branch. A hummingbird feeder just outside the glass can be more entertaining than a rented movie. When children see your enthusiasm, they will respond with excitement. Let them grow a tomato plant and share its bright fruit with family. Children who have been led to discover the intricate and dynamic marvels of nature will appreciate their own vital role in sustaining their world as adults.

While traveling in Europe, I loved to see the open windows of houses, airing bedding in a bracing Alpine breeze. Perhaps one of the simplest, most healthful gestures we can make is to open windows. Yes, of course, we can simply control our indoor climate by adjusting a thermostat, but stale indoor air

Nothing will banish the blahs more quickly than a walk outdoors.

becomes more healthful with fresh infusions. Consider the number of chemicals we release into our homes daily—cleaning products, disinfectants, glass cleaners, furniture polishes, detergents, bleaching agents, insecticides, room fresheners, hair sprays, aerosol deodorants, and chlorine steam from showers. When we begin to enumerate the sources of indoor pollution, we may find ourselves examining these products. How many of them do we really need? Can we replace petrochemicals with safer plant-based alternatives? Environmentally sound options are increasingly available. Additionally, throwing open windows will not only circulate fresh air, but will make us feel closer to the cadences of the seasons.

Why stop there? Since we are raising our windows and health consciousness, let us look beyond what we breathe and glance at personal care products—the shampoos, lotions, cosmetics, and other chemicals which we apply to our skin and hair. Although human skin is a natural barrier to disease, it is also porous. Whatever we apply to our exterior is absorbed and migrates to our interior. More healthful, plant-based choices are worth investigating in this category as well. And, of course, chemicals of any kind impact our planet. If we want to increase our awareness of the world about us, a good place to begin may be with our own homes and bodies.

Leo Tolstoy holds that "one of the first conditions of happiness is that the link between Man and Nature shall not be broken." We can easily say that nature is important to us, but what comforts and conveniences are we willing to give up to demonstrate our respect for the world in which we live? We seldom consider the cost to our earth and its inhabitants of creating, advertising, transporting, selling, using, and disposing of goods. We feel entitled to our excess while ignoring the damage from our growing greed. Nature will not recover indefinitely. Reducing our demands and desires, choosing wisely, reusing and recycling will demonstrate our commitment and connection to nature. Becoming close to the earth, sensitive to it, aware of it as our source of life, and committed to its maintenance and purity will generate reverence for the only world we have. Let us rethink our sacred obligation to what God's hand has made. Wendell Berry entreats our esteem: "The care of the Earth is our most ancient and most worthy, and after all our most pleasing responsibility. To cherish what remains of it and to foster its renewal is our only hope."

Passion

" I still find each day too short for all the thoughts I want to think, all the walks I want to take, all the books I want to read and all the friends I want to see." John Burroughs expresses how we feel about our passions. What makes your own pulse race, your feet fly, your mind quicken, your heart thrill? Pursue it. Embrace it. Do it.

Sometimes inconvenient passions claim us. An unforgettable oversize painting, a book we have no time to read, a relationship which requires tending, or an outreach we do not need. What become our passions do not always fit into our plans. But it is worth assuming those ardors which tug at the heart. What we truly love will always find a place in our homes and in our lives.

Poet Stanley Kunitz poses a question and answers it: "What makes the engine go? / Desire, desire, desire." Unfortunately, infatuations can be hard to distinguish from enduring passions. An intimate relationship with God can help us to determine what is best for us. Talking with Him and listening to His responses will guide our enthusiasms. "Delight yourself in the Lord," reads Psalm 37:4, "and he will give you the desires of your heart."

The passionate woman has a keen curiosity, an eager intellect, a lively interest in others, zeal for excellence, devotion to her God and family, fervor for service, an earnest pursuit of significance, and ebullient optimism. Designer Yves Saint Laurent agrees, "The most beautiful make-up of a woman is passion."

Patience

D o not be afraid to go bare . . . your rooms and gardens that is . . . until you encounter what you love. I looked for twenty years of our marriage to find a bed for our master bedroom, and, after fifteen years in our current home, I am still searching for the right antique cabinet for a narrow spot in the kitchen. Rooms, gardens, and wardrobes are expensive and enduring design endeavors. They require building deliberately on carefully selected foundations. Instead of beginning with complete and matching suites, acquire little by little over the years, leaving plenty of space for new discoveries—an unusual antique lamp, hardy species of plant, or perfect jacket. By taking time, investing in what is wonderful, instead of hurrying to fill a void, a room, yard, or closet can evolve by layers into a lasting satisfaction.

When my second book, *A Fragrant Fullness*, was being published, the graphic artist sent me a proof for the book's cover, a hodge-podge of tiny images of various scented items. The busy cover offered no appeal to potential readers, who would not have been able to decipher its images without squinting. I returned it with a request for an elegant cover with a single dominant flower image. Soon I received the revised cover, this time beautiful yellow tulips, an eye-catching photograph which would compel readers to reach for the book. Unfortunately, tulips are not recognized for their scent. Although I was eager to see the book in print and reluctant to further delay publication, I returned the second cover attempt with a listing of fragrant flower possibilities. The third effort was perfect, lovely pink roses on a background of sumptuous green leaves. I could almost smell the blossoms. While an author has to relinquish much control in matters of book construction, the cover was a significant component of the book that I needed to be right. I am glad I persisted.

Getting it right may take longer than we may like. But, as the German proverb assures us, "Long is not forever." Holding out for

the right choice often means only a small cost of time for a significant exchange of much greater value.

I like this aphorism's vivid image of time's transformative power: "Patience—in time the grass becomes milk." Gardens are great lessons in patience. From a bedding plant only a few inches tall, we have, years later, a sprawling bay bush which provides more leaves than we can begin to use. We share them with chef friends, use them in stews, shred them fresh into simmering dishes, dry branches and tie them to kitchen gifts, or fill jars with leaves for holiday giving. Like other garden delights, our bay offers its aromatic largess with little more investment than time.

Waiting for a traffic light to turn, for a computer to complete a function, for a microwave to heat, or for the shopper ahead to make her transaction takes only as much time as watching a spider spin a filament, icicles drip and puddle, or a bee dip a blossom for nectar. But our impatience reflects our attitude. We are rushing through the uninspiring tasks of driving, computing, cooking, and shopping, focused on something else ahead. Watching the spider, or icicle, or bee captures our attention in the moment, and time seems suspended. Our sense of hurry falls away.

Of course, we cannot be fully in each moment when our minds must handle multiple matters, when we need to finish a report, beat the school bell, pick up groceries, and get a casserole on the table before baseball practice within the next hour, but we can be attentive to our attitude while scrambling through demands and duties. And we want to be particularly conscious that we are not rushing through meaningful moments, which do demand that we put down the phone, remote control, or laundry basket and give our full attention to our spouse or child who needs to talk.

Hurrying through all the demands that crowd our days can make us irritable and easily angered. And if we "gave at the office" the best of our time and energies, we may have only a frazzled remnant of ourselves to share with the most valuable priority in our lives—those we love. Could we not train ourselves to savor moments as they unfold, to consciously consider the importance of the child's fear, the husband's concern, the co-worker's personal burden that may require a bit more from us just now, or our own desire for reflection? These are the matters of consequence that comprise our life, and give us pause. "Let patience have her perfect work" (James 1:4a, *NKJV*).

Rushing to a medical appointment, I am stopped in traffic waiting for a train to pass. My mind wanders to slower childhood days when our family watched trains rattle through our little Midwestern community, hinting of the distant and exotic briefly passing our way. These leisurely moments must have begun my romance with trains. As teenagers, my sisters and I rode one of the

last passenger trains to the neighboring cattle town of Abilene, just
for the fading experience. When starting out after college, I took
the train to visit friends a state away. While living in Europe during
my husband Michael's military career, we found trains our preferred
mode of travel. We could observe the countryside, take a sleeping
car if the trip were long, and be delivered right to the city center.
Without the stress of driving, we could enjoy a book, a glass of wine,
relaxed conversation, or nap to the rhythm of the rails. My mind
drifted to train tunnels where we stole the kisses of young marriage.
In a French village, while we waited on a rail-side bench, the arrival
of our train threw from the tracks a great spray of snow. Serenity
descended in a cloud of tingling powder which settled on our lids
and lips and laps. . . .

My reverie interrupted, cross bars rise and the train ahead of me
passes from view. I find myself no longer rushed, but grateful for the
pause to follow my nostalgic train of thought. In the words of poet
Mary Oliver, "No gift greater than ecstasy, unless it's patience."

An increasing number of people are living to very old age.
In my parent's youth, people routinely died in their 40s and 50s.
Today, reaching one's 90s is not unusual. Oldsters claim among
their secrets of longevity, eating oatmeal, drinking water,
hard work, exercise, spouses, pets, and genes. From observation,
I would add to this list, patience—calm acceptance of life's
vicissitudes. Many of those who endure seem to take all in stride.
They are not hurried by unmet demands, but focused on the task
before them. They are not charmed by appeals of the distant, but
content with the near at hand. They are not frazzled by over-
commitment, but assume what they can capably handle. They are
not fretful about the future, but present in the moment. Instead,
they follow Virgil's perfect daily prescription: "Endure, and preserve
yourself for better things."

Considering a purchase, a choice, a solution? Most consequential decisions benefit from time. We might be surprised at how much we gain by allowing leisure to sift, examine, evaluate, and clarify. Judgment seems to improve with even one day's wait. The best approach to decision? Pray for direction; then sleep on it. And keep in mind that answers may not be immediate. "Never think that God's delays are God's denials," says Georges-Louis Leclerc. "Hold on; hold fast; hold out. Patience is genius."

PRAY FOR DIRECTION; THEN SLEEP ON IT. How hard the waiting can be . . . on a boss' response, creeping traffic, a trip for which we are saving, a teenager's late return, lab results, healing. Why do we hate to wait? Inconvenience? Delayed gratification? Fear? Our patience muscle requires conscious effort to exercise and develop. But the regular workout is worth it. Patience is not only a virtue; it is the virtue from which all other virtues stem—kindness, forgiveness, charity. Gautama Buddha views patience as the "greatest prayer," so let us move it to the top of our prayer list, then pause for God's reply. What are we waiting for?

Perspective

When decorating rooms, play musical chairs. Sit at various places in a room and focus on what is visible from different angles—not just in the room, but through doorways into other spaces. A lamp shade near a reading spot may need adjusting for a low chair. A table may need to be closer to hold a book or drink. Draperies may need shifting to prevent a glare.

Is a kitchen counter mess obvious from the dining area? Hang a lightweight scrim on a ceiling track to pull at mealtime. Is a private vanity open to a bedroom? Use louvered doors or a foldable screen. Is the view from an entry unpleasant? Place planters just beyond the doorway and install evergreens. A line of sight should be as attractive as surroundings. Our point of view matters.

I made my modest morning walk around the neighborhood parkway in faded leggings and no special T-shirt. She raced toward me, power-walking with weights in a cute coordinated exercise outfit, matching headband, and the latest athlete-endorsed shoes. Breezing past, she asked, "How many miles do you walk?" I had never thought to measure distance.

Her question made me consider how intent we are at measuring—how much education, how much income, how many achievements, how many acquisitions, how much recognition, how many friends, how much cost, how much gain. What really matters, we cannot quantify—how much happiness, how much kindness, how much giving, how much good? Zelda Fitzgerald points out, "Nobody has ever measured, even poets, how much a heart can hold." Besides, the amount of effort we make will not determine our destination. Our promise of Paradise is a gift of faith. We will never be asked how far we traveled to heaven, but rather, whether we exercised love along the way.

Our storm windows were horrid, cleaning them impossible. Those awful contraptions groaned and jammed, bit knuckles and broke nails with any effort to raise or lower them. Even a professional cleaning company could not handle them without a terrible fight. It became too much. I left them smudged, spotted, and smeared, pulled the blinds and ignored them. There are just some things we have to let go. If we cannot see out of our circumstances, we can, at least, change our outlook.

The familiar adage, "This too shall pass" is usually applied to adversity, but the good times pass at the same rate as the bad. Do we have family, friends, health, work? Instead of waiting for them to become ideal, we can enjoy them even when they are less than perfect. Bliss Carman inspires us to focus on beauty inherent in the present and its potential for the future: "Lord of the far horizons / Give us the eyes to see / Over the verge of the sundown / The beauty that is to be."

> *If* WE CANNOT SEE OUT OF OUR CIRCUMSTANCES, WE CAN, AT LEAST, CHANGE OUR OUTLOOK.

What makes us most anxious? Our worries? They may never occur or be as troubling as we imagine. Should consequence arise, we will deal with them then. Our fears? We can identify what frightens us and overcome our dread. Our mistakes? These usually cannot be undone, but we can forgive ourselves, learn from them, and move on. Our responsibilities? They will always await us. My sister Jolene thanks God each evening for just enough hours in the day to accomplish what most needed doing. When we feel uneasy, praying that we may see the long view helps.

The French have a saying, "Tout casse, tout passe, tout lasse"— everything breaks, everything passes, nothing lasts. While discovering the impermanence of what we love can hurt, learning to relinquish control can also bear comfort. The words of Robert Frost hearten us: "In three words I can sum up everything I've learned about life: It goes on."

If we stand on a beach or on an unimpeded plain and survey the distance, the vista before us will eventually disappear into the horizon. So will our lives. What will matter in a day, a week, a month, a year, when our children grow up, when we are gone and remembered? At the end of life, the promotion, the stunningly decorated home, the world travel, or the days packed with activity will not matter. To evaluate the worth of how we spend our time, we simply need to ask, "What will it ultimately matter?" Are we improving our relationships to one another and to God? These will endure beyond the vanishing point at the end of the world.

Although we often think of eternity as commencing after we die, it has already begun for us in the here and now. Occasionally we glimpse the glories God originally intended for us, which will be fully realized in the hereafter. Elizabeth Barrett Browning encourages us to open our eyes to common splendors: "Earth's crammed with heaven, / And every common bush afire with God: / But only he who sees, takes off his shoes."

Although God created us in perfect grace with Him, sin eroded our relationship with Him, with others, and with our world. The damage is evident. But in Christ, God redeemed us, through faith, to eternal life. Manifestations of God's grace surround us. If we are still and receptive, fully engaged in each rare, elusive day, we may savor those sacred moments. When we pet a husband, nibble a cat, bask in the steam of a fragrant cup, we glimpse forever . . . today. A favorite passage of mine from John Burroughs reads, "One of the hardest lessons we have to learn in this life, and one that many persons never learn, is to see the divine, the celestial, the pure, in the common, the near at hand—to see that heaven lies about us here in this world."

As my flight emerges from the clouds and a miniature landscape appears—small fields, small houses, a small lake, small buildings, all so insignificant. From high above the vastness of our populated sphere, I recognize that somewhere I cannot see, a patient waits for a diagnosis, a worker confronts a new challenge, a soldier engages in battle, a student takes a test—monumental moments to each, and yet, each so small in the grand design. The plane leans and casts its small shadow on a small patch of our small planet. I see my life from a less significant perspective, and marvel that I matter so much to God.

Planning

What is the point of entertaining if you cannot enjoy your own party? When you are occupied all evening in the kitchen, hustling back and forth from the dinner table, or frantically dashing to refill glasses, neither you nor your guests feel comfortable. Planning ahead makes entertaining a breeze. Invite guests approximately a month in advance so they can reserve the date on their calendars. A week or two ahead, plan the menu and make a grocery list of ingredients. Several days before, shop for groceries and begin cooking. Create a menu with dishes that can be prepared beforehand, so you will not be fussing when guests arrive. Make ahead dishes that can be frozen or refrigerated. The day before, set the table and arrange a bar area where guests can help themselves. Unless you are entertaining the President or Pope, leave deep cleaning until afterwards; simply tidy surfaces and clean the bathroom.

On the day of the party, all that will be left to do is flower arranging, limited final cooking, and last minute details. Planning ahead will leave time to find provocative subjects in the newspaper for invigorating conversation starters. W.S. Gilbert's advice is valid: "When planning a dinner party, what's more important than what's on the table is what's on the chairs." Long after the evening, no one will be able to describe the food, but they will recall the people and occasion, the stories and talk. Finally, indulge in a dinner party's most important element . . . an afternoon nap.

Among my recipe files, I keep dinner party records. A separate card for each occasion indicates the date, guests, menu (successes and failures), and perhaps even snapshots of table setting and decoration. These records help to avoid repetition and inspire new ideas for entertaining.

Planning is requisite in the garden, too. Although buying favorite plants, plunking them into the ground, and hoping for the best may be easier, a lot of time and expense can be saved by proceeding deliberately. If you are uncertain, professional advice can be valuable

at all stages of garden design. Begin with small projects, working on a manageable area at a time. Gardening is hard work, time consuming, and expensive. Begin by testing and augmenting soil. This is not the glamorous aspect of gardening, but it may be the most important in terms of a garden's beauty, longevity, and ease of maintenance later. Browse local gardens, books, and web sites for inspiration. Select attractive plants suitable to your climate. For hardiness, choose native plants when possible. Check sun exposures of planting sites. Do you need plants for afternoon shade, full sun, or filtered light? Note water requirements of plants and be sure to provide a reliable and sufficient water source for the site. Avoid overcrowding. Determine plants' mature size, and allow room for growth. Mulch heavily. By carefully tending to all the preliminaries, you can sit back to enjoy years of garden delight.

In our own back yard, I envisioned banks of blooms, a shaded pergola, stone paths meandering through manicured beds, stately statuary, and the soughing of water. My imagination did not extend to who would install this dream, maintain it, or pay for it. Instead, friends brought us a peach tree, shrubs salvaged from a grading job, and a swing. We made room for vegetables and have accommodated encroaching shade as trees mature. When I look at our back yard now, it looks nothing like I may have fancied. With little coherent design, it has evolved in unexpected ways.

We can seldom implement a plan precisely or entirely. Unpredictable elements, growth, and change revise our scheme. Over time, a plan may no longer suit us or our circumstances and must be tossed to accommodate what we have at hand. If we are going to make a plan, we should plan on making adjustments. Rainer Maria Rilke invites us to embrace uncertainty: "Be patient toward all that is unsolved in your heart and try to love the questions themselves."

Goals can be valuable for our career, our finances, even for our personal, religious, or family life. We can more readily reach them by setting specific and realistic goals, establishing a target for completion, identifying steps to achievement, and planning a reward for accomplishment. Setting goals and steps to achieve them can get us started, establish priorities, direct us, motivate us along the way, and, ultimately, make us successful in our effort. Abraham Lincoln knew the importance of preparation: "I will study and get ready and someday my chance will come."

For earlier generations, life was expectedly brief, and, before widespread availability of medications, death was often painful. Why do we fear death so much today, even though our life expectancy is longer and we have means for more comfortable ends? Perhaps we feel less fulfilled because we live so preoccupied with the present. Perhaps we want to maintain control, failing to recognize how much remains beyond our power. Perhaps we dread diminished strength and abilities. Perhaps we are apprehensive about what lies beyond the familiar and known. Despite our best plans, finally we must recognize life's impermanence, learn to relinquish our hold here, and grasp God's extended hand. ✐

Practice

My heart sank as I overheard a farm mother describing to my own the glories of her children's involvement with 4-H. I had seen these country kids in barns at the county fair, mucking the stalls of cows and hogs. I wanted no part of it.

But before we could say, "Head, heart, hands, and health," there we were on a Wednesday night in the basement of a rural one-room school, reciting the 4-H pledge to a clover-leaf flag and singing from battered song books, "Sons of the Soil are We." Lyrics had obviously not been adapted to city girls.

We were enrolled in baking and sewing, which sounded marginally better than livestock. Surely my sister and I could whip up a cake and sew a stitch or two. Still, I could feel summer freedom slipping away.

From a jovial, yeasty woman with a reputation for breaking high-spirited horses and baking high-rising breads, we learned how to measure and mix ingredients, punch and shape dough to make crescent rolls. A smaller, more serious mother with yardsticks showed us how to read the hieroglyphics on a pattern envelope, figure yardage, find the grain of fabric, and assemble a puzzle of pattern pieces on material.

When school let out for summer, efforts for the county fair began in earnest. The kitchen was a flurry of spoons and bowls, spilled flour and broken eggs, as we tried one cookie recipe after another in search of a prize winner. Our best and most beautiful cookie specimens were carefully wrapped and frozen.

My mother, a talented seamstress herself, guided our first sewing attempts—a square table cloth and napkins, advancing to an apron with a pocket. The beginner projects were not as simple as they sounded. We stitched and ripped and ripped and stitched in a blur of frustrated tears to sew perfect seams that would earn judges' approval and coveted ribbons. My mother, in her infinite patience, could not have foreseen the emotional challenge of steering pre-teen girls to perfection. Half-finished pieces were screamed at, balled, and thrown into a corner, only to be retrieved when our senses returned. Mother smoothed feelings and fabric. We tried again. Finally satisfied, we ironed our precious labors for the pre-fair fashion show. At the big event, we walked the runway in our gingham aprons as proudly as the older girls who modeled tailored suits.

My mother, in her infinite patience, could not have foreseen the emotional challenge of steering pre-teen girls to perfection.

Fair day was a frenzy of last minute baking, toting entries to hot fairgrounds while keeping frosting from weeping, checking out the competition, and watching judges as they tasted cakes, peered at stitches, and paged through our dutiful project reports. Everyone got ribbons. Though we all knew the vast gap between paltry white and state-champion purple, we complimented each other.

Between fairs, we served as officers of our club, learning how to write minutes, keep books, and conduct parliamentary procedure, mostly a matter of getting to the end of a meeting as quickly as possible. Recruited for regional competitions, we suffered nauseous backseat trips to spend Saturday in a stuffy gym, waiting our turn to present a custard-baking demonstration.

When fall's first essay required an account of how we spent our vacation, we may not have counted our 4-H hours as summer fun. But when I collaborate on a project, speak before a crowd, or persist until a task is done well, I am silently grateful for all those young experiences that gave my life straight seams and sweet rewards.

Practice is a matter of trial and effort. We cultivate competence by regularity and routine. Can't we hear our mothers' persistent refrain? "Stand straight, sit still, practice your scales, and behave." Whether we are perfecting posture, piano, or virtue, persistence is paramount. We cannot expect to master a skill, a talent, or a vocation until we have attempted, failed, revised, and repeated again and again and again. "Try again. Fail again. Fail better," exhorts Samuel Beckett. Proficiency does not occur overnight, but over a lifetime. When Pablo Casals was 94, he was asked why he was still practicing three hours a day. He responded, "I'm beginning to notice some improvement."

Though I seldom hear the word acedia used, I feel it more often than I would wish. Acedia is spiritual torpor or apathy. I feel it when I am not spending enough time attending to my spirituality. I become cranky, self-centered, cynical, discouraged, and distracted. I do not even notice how inadequate and unreliable my own resources are until a relationship snaps, or I sink into doldrums, and I finally realize I need some spiritual refreshment. I fall asleep praying, I seem out of touch with God, I find it easy to skip religious services, even when I need them most. But a return to regular worship helps me to see how spiritual matters in my life are being resolved. From day to day, I may not notice whether I am really developing that virtue of kindness which I have been trying to improve, or whether the concern I have shared with God is resolving, but a weekly time set aside for ongoing re-evaluation helps me to renew my commitment and gives me inspiration to persist.

Teachers know students attend classes because they are obligated to successfully complete a course to earn a grade or a degree. We hope they will, additionally, gain enlightenment and proficiency. When my college students miss class, they often ask when they return, "Did I miss anything?" I wonder if they think we sat quietly with our hands folded waiting for their return. How do I begin to enumerate all that transpired in their absence?

When we are absent from religious services, what do we miss? Great mysteries—speaking directly to God, hearing God's voice speak to us, becoming intimately acquainted and engaging in sacred union with the divine, nourishing our souls, mingling with a community that shares our faith, finding inspiration for the week ahead, receiving a sacred blessing. Maybe such mystical moments could happen anywhere, just as education can occur outside the

WE WILL ALWAYS MAKE TIME TO PURSUE WHAT WE LOVE MOST. classroom, but why not be physically present in the setting which can best avail such riches?

We will always make time to pursue what we love most. Attending a house of worship is like visiting an art gallery, museum, or musical performances—we go not just to enjoy the spectacle, but to bask in God's glory, to experience His grace, and to hone our spiritual sensibilities.

As a dancer, Martha Graham knew what mastery requires: "Practice means to perform, over and over again in the face of all obstacles, some act of vision, of faith, of desire. Practice is a means of inviting the perfection desired."

Privacy

D iogenes defines blushing as "the color of virtue." But little
seems to cause discomfort today. Tell-all television, revealing
fashions, computer exposure, cell phone conversations spilling
intimacies—all fail to raise eyebrows. Why do we expect to share our
lives indiscriminately and then wonder why our privacy is invaded?
While quick and facile confidences with strangers invite indiscretion,
reserve and reticence can preserve a comfortable distance. Besides, a
hint of mystery is always alluring.

Jesus often retired to solitary places—to a desert, a garden, hills.
He needed to rest from demands of the day, to quiet his thoughts, to
contemplate his work, and to converse with his Father. We often seem
insistent on crowding our days with contacts, surrounding ourselves
with people, uncomfortable being apart from others. Are we afraid
of being alone with our turbulent selves, apprehensive about what
our heart may reveal, or fearful of what God may say to us? William
Wordsworth expresses the satisfaction of time alone: "When from our

better selves we have too long / Been parted by the hurrying world, and droop, / Sick of its business, of its pleasures tired, / How gracious, how benign is solitude."

SOLITUDE MAY BE ONE OF THE SIMPLEST, YET MOST PROFOUND, FORMS OF REFRESHMENT.

Solitude may be one of the simplest, yet most profound, forms of refreshment. George Herbert advocates being alone to "see what thy soul doth wear," to tend internal realms. Away from the congestion of company, we can focus more clearly on restorative pursuits—music, books, prayer, painting, gardening, or day dreaming. With no one to distract or demand, we can clear our minds and revive our flagging spirits. I share Voltaire's opinion that "the happiest of all lives is a busy solitude." If we are unable to find a time or place to be alone daily, however briefly, we can carve out solitary time at least once a week, informing family and friends when we will be unavailable. Once those closest to us recognize how vital our time alone is, they will honor our commitment and reap the benefits of our renewal. "There is a quality to being alone that is incredibly precious," writes Anne Morrow Lindbergh. "Life rushes back into the void, richer, more vivid, fuller than before."

Quality

W ell-intentioned guests may remark, "You shouldn't have gone to so much bother." Rubbish! The comment recognizes the work rather than the pleasure and satisfaction of extra effort. Do bother. Set a pretty table for no special evening, put a single exquisite flower in a vase on your bedside table . . . or your husband's, dress as though you are going somewhere—you are! Of course we should bother. As years advance, we may be unable to make the efforts we wish. How many lifetimes will we have to bother?

Not so long ago, travelers dressed up for air travel, and patients polished their appearance for a dental appointment. Today all manner of dishevelment is evident anywhere we go. Has our sense of propriety devolved so quickly? At some point, decorum developed a faint whiff of rigidity, and began to dissolve. Formality may have lost credence, but not its cachet. Appearance still matters. While we may live differently today, comfortable is no excuse for sloppy. Plenty of comfortable, good-looking options exist, costing nothing more than untidy choices do.

Looking our best really does alter the way people respond to us. When we dress neat and trig, service is often more attentive. And who matters more to us than those at home who see us most often? Even alone when no one is looking, dressing well makes us feel good about ourselves. "Dress," notes Voltaire, "changes the manners." Elegance is not dressing to impress, it is an innate soigné attitude—sophisticated and well groomed.

What do you wear most often? Casual jeans? Fine, but trade the faded, stretched, and frayed favorites for a well-proportioned, appropriate length, well-maintained pair. Swap the sweatshirt for a neat pull-over or turtle-neck. What about that ratty robe and nightgown? Something you wear so often is worth a tasteful investment. At work, a few well-tailored professional outfits present a better image than a closet full of ill-fitting, dowdy, or trendy apparel which has outlived its life expectancy.

Tailoring may be one of the best investments of any wardrobe: pants hemmed to height and comfortable through the stride; blouses and jackets with appropriate shoulder width, sleeves in proportion to arm length, a bodice skimming one's curves; skirts fit to the waist with ease through the hips, lined for body, and a length to flatter legs. Madeleine Vionnet advises, "The dress must not hang on the body, but follow its lines. It must accompany its wearer, and when a woman

smiles, the dress must smile with her." Alterations can be pricey, but when you are comfortable in well-fitting clothes, you will not seek replacements as often and will save in the long run. Look sharp. You will feel the elegant edge.

Our European immersion has led me to value quality rather than quantity. The Continental attitude is less acquisitive, more discriminating. It involves a mindful attention to aesthetics and an unhurried pace to savor them. A proclivity for quality permeates even the mundane—selecting flawless plums to create an artscape in an antique bowl, indulging in fine stationery for a heartfelt note to a friend, replacing a scrap paper bookmark with a husband's lovingly selected birthday card. Everyday refinements distinguish the modest and imbue the simple with significance.

Quality applies to our activities as well. We may not have the means to attend regular live performances of opera, ballet, or theatre, but we need not settle for entertainment pabulum. Fine arts can be affordable. Televised arts programming allows viewers to sample music classics, to see art masterpieces, and to travel through history. Often museums and galleries offer afternoons open to the public at no charge. Volunteering as a docent or an usher might enable one to see exhibits or performances in exchange. Local colleges and universities have busy calendars of art shows, musical and theatrical performances. By availing ourselves of cultural opportunities, we can cultivate our artistic tastes and our appreciation for the creative spirit. We may even be motivated to take a class and experience the thrill for ourselves. Kurt Vonnegut indicates the potential in artistic pursuit: "To practice any art, no matter how well or badly, is a way to make your soul grow."

Whatever we do, it is worth doing to the best of our ability. "Quality is never an accident," contends John Ruskin. "It is always the result of intelligent effort." When we invest our effort with excellence, the result is an expression of dignity.

Quiet

The first year of our marriage on Christmas morning in Germany, we rode an empty streetcar to downtown Heidelberg. The historic city's usually crowded main street was completely deserted. For the entire length of the cobblestone pedestrian way, not a single soul had yet appeared to leave a footprint in deep overnight snow. Our breath forming puffs of exhilaration and awe, we trudged for blocks to the muffled crunch of snow, alone in an Old World dream of ancient buildings, cathedral spires, and an imposing castle in hills beyond. Emerging from our reverie, we caught a glimmer of light from heavy paned windows and a trail of smoke rising from the restaurant's chimney. We shook the chill and snow from hats, scarves, and coats, then found a seat beside the ceramic stove, where our boots thawed in puddles. Sipping warm soup that reverent morning, we tasted a silence too sacred for words.

In the Alsace region of France, we visited Mont Sainte Odile for another muted interlude. Our drive through green vistas ascended to the mountaintop abbey, where words felt irreverent in the ancient spiritual sanctuary, footsteps echoing from stone, the ethereal voices of nuns raised in vespers. With the sisters, we shared a silent supper of boiled eggs, young spinach, and new potatoes from their garden. From our room's treetop balcony, we marveled at the spectacular view beyond. When a crashing, thunderous storm shook windows to wake us from night's sweet oblivion, we watched the flashing heavens in awed oblation, then yielded to the muffled down of dreams.

Marcel Proust describes the rooms of his home as "saturated with the bouquet of silence." I share his taste for this sweet hush. Quiet is my own favorite essence in a room. In fact, I thrive on it. Inspiration often taps a writer's shoulder when the mind is at ease. New ideas arrive with greatest clarity while I shower, iron, or drift to sleep, as if surfacing in clear waters. I keep note paper throughout the house, in my car, and stashed in my purse to capture thoughts for sorting and exploring later. The best ideas, solutions, and approaches often seem to arrive unsolicited when the mind is unoccupied. In stillness, we are more receptive and attentive to the vital, neglected dimensions of our lives and souls. In quiet expectation, we can reflect and transcend. Mother Teresa affirms, "God speaks in the silence of the heart. Listening is the beginning of prayer."

How much information do we need? What do we truly need to know? And how quickly do we need to know? Our society's information overload has been described as analogous to sipping water from a fire hose. I prefer to turn off the flood of what passes for broadcast news. Rather than sit captive through 30 minutes of unsettling headlines, subjected for half that time to commercials for products that create anxiety—Should I be taking this medicine? cleaning my house? getting more insurance?—I could leisurely read a newspaper with a cup of tea, selecting what I want and need to know at the depth and pace I desire.

We have lost touch with Bertrand Russell's sentiment that "a happy life must be to a great extent a quiet life, for it is only in an atmosphere of quiet that true joy can live." Our attention spans are programmed by the staccato clamor of computers, electronics, and disjointed disruptions of commercial television. The sonic overload of technology makes us uncomfortable with stillness. Not only can we not hear ourselves think, we cannot think. But quiet activities, like reading, talking with a spouse, playing with children, gardening, or walking can encourage mindfulness. In a muted calm, problems, challenges, dilemmas are more easily resolved. An unexpected word, person, or occurrence may bear an insight missed in a cacophonous moment. When we muffle noise, we can embrace the gentle melody of a crackling fire, gurgling fountain, or laughter bubbling across a wine glass. We feel our nerves and shoulders relax. Listening to wind chimes, classical music, or whispers in bed, we are soon enveloped in our own thoughts' easy echo.

"A HAPPY LIFE MUST BE TO A GREAT EXTENT A QUIET LIFE, FOR IT IS ONLY IN AN ATMOSPHERE OF QUIET THAT TRUE JOY CAN LIVE."

A patter of paws, a coyote's call, shifting ashes, thunder's prelude, a toddler's squeal, a soughing breeze, geese above, Mother's far voice, sister's piano, a distant train, tolling bells, laughing friends, sheep afield, my husband's sleeping breath beside me—I want to listen now and listen well, to store these sacred sounds against the day when only their echo remains.

Reading

When browsing decorating magazines, I use my magnifying glass to read the spines of books on pictured shelves and tables. Titles tell me about a room's inhabitants, about their preferences and passions. We are what we read. Lady M. W. Montagu's sentiment remains true today: "No entertainment is so cheap as reading, nor any pleasure so lasting."

The irony of reading is that a solitary occupation should so enlarge space, time, and the reader's mind. Henry Miller recommends that "we should read to give our souls a chance to luxuriate." A book can transport us beyond our rooms wherein we read to far and exotic locales, propel us in an instant to other dimensions of past and future, and engage us in ideas and manners of thinking we had not known existed nor would have considered possible. How black symbols on a white page can accomplish such breathtaking feats is an awesome mystery.

A friend of mine quips that everything she knows about life she has learned from novels. Regardless of what we read—biography, self-help, mystery, romance, history, poetry, travel, or inspiration— we will reflect on what is important to us, measure new experiences against our own value system, consider, evaluate, accept, reject, or modify what confronts us. My friend is right—reading is a fine way to learn about life . . . and about ourselves. Ralph Waldo Emerson expresses the enlightenment: "In every work of genius, we recognize our own rejected thoughts; they come back to us with a certain alienated majesty."

What should we read? The beauty of reading is that we are not held to "shoulds." We can read what we love, what appeals to our idiosyncratic interests, dusty books that may not have been checked out of the library for years. We are not obliged to read best sellers geared to mass tastes. A wide variety of books

READING IS A FINE WAY TO LEARN ABOUT LIFE . . . AND ABOUT OURSELVES.

is increasingly accessible. Even small towns today often have access to state-wide interlibrary loan systems, expanding local collections and making our hardest choice what to read next.

To flex intellectual muscles, to expand exposure, and to discover new areas of interest, read a newspaper article each day on a subject that may not interest you. A simple taste of information will prompt attention to related headlines and soon encourage reading about unfamiliar subjects in greater depth, cultivating opinions and tastes, and seeking books to explore new enthusiasms. Henry Wadsworth Longfellow praises the bliss of reading: "The love of learning, the sequestered nooks, / And all the sweet serenity of books."

You can give your family, or yourself, no greater gift than encouragement and opportunities to read. Keep books, magazines, and newspapers about, visit the library and bookstores together, read yourself, and talk about books. Stretch children's reading skills by reading to them books beyond their current reading level. My own childhood grounding in the King James Version of The Bible enriched my vocabulary and gave me an appreciation for the sound and artistry of language. Read passages, articles, and stories aloud to your spouse or children, even if they roll their eyes. Soon they will find reading delights to share with you in return. I espouse the philosophy of Margaret Fuller Ossoli: "A house is no home unless it contains food and fire for the mind as well as for the body."

Students who desire the fast track to completing a degree often wonder why the study of literature is a college requirement. What practical application can literature possibly have to their future careers as engineers, accountants, or nurses? But as they read mossy classics to edgy contemporary works from cultures around the globe, they begin to recognize universal subjects and themes. Readers become absorbed in experiences unlike their own; they see the world

from new perspectives; they contemplate the thoughts of others; they are entertained, inspired, and edified; they marvel at the capabilities of language. Why do we read challenging works from antiquity as well as popular page-turners? To determine what matters and why, to understand our responsibilities to our earth and its creatures, to explore relationships, to determine what is ethical, to make us fully human. "In reading," finds Stéphane Mallarmé "a lonely quiet concert is given to our minds; all our mental faculties will be present in this symphonic exaltation."

Books are incomparable companions. By stimulating our own thoughts, the company of books encourages us not only to enjoy our own company, but also to become good company—informed, engaged, and stimulating. Finally, reading enables us to transcend the temporal. In fact, Jorge Luis Borges reveals his own vision: "I have always believed that paradise will be a kind of library."

The Ridiculous

Some homeowners display their sense of humor to passers-by. En route to the university each morning through a staid, exclusive neighborhood, I pass the home of an irreverent resident. In her living room window poses a department store dress mannequin decked in exotic seasonal outfits—glittering streamers and a martini glass for the New Year, theatrical mask and beads for Mardi Gras, dotty golf togs for the Masters Tournament, or a Carmen Miranda costume for sheer caprice.

In a lighted Christmas display further north, Santa in his sleigh reins a phalanx of pink flamingos. From a snow bank, the flamingo out front flashes Rudolph's familiar red nose, eliciting drifts of laughter. Cultivating a sense of humor can reveal fun in the most unexpected ways, and Agnes Strickland considers that "next to the virtue, the fun in this world is what we can least spare."

Did you know that in one of the earliest published French versions of the Cinderella tale, her glass slippers were red velvet mules encrusted with pearls, reflecting the fashion of Louis XIV's court? Or that in Frank Baum's original story of Oz, Dorothy's magic shoes were silver? They were changed to red in *The Wizard of Oz* film for cinematic impact. Just in case I need to return quickly to my native state of Kansas, like Dorothy, I have my own pair of ruby slippers beside my door for a fast get-away. They bring to mind the words of G. K. Chesterton: "Angels can fly because they take themselves lightly."

One tenet of my personal decorating philosophy holds that every room should include elements of both the sublime and the ridiculous— something wonderful, but also something odd or outrageous, fanciful or fantastic. Among my eccentricities are a bench upholstered in an old

If WE CAN TAKE OURSELVES LESS SERIOUSLY, WE WILL FIND LEVITY IN OUR OWN FOOLISHNESS, AND LIGHTNESS OF HEART. tapestry of kittens wearing shirts and dresses, peering over a garden fence. Elsewhere, a petrified chameleon peers from dried flowers; a toothy alligator buttresses books; an Aladdinesque lamp awaits a rub and a wish. Rooms and their occupants respond to fun infusions. William Makepeace Thackeray recognizes that "a good laugh is sunshine in a house."

Jewelry is not immune to silliness. Finding veterinary records of former pet inoculations, I linked outdated rabies tags on a chain to create a whimsical charm bracelet. Wearing it recalls our feline pals and makes me giggle. Life is filled with absurdities. Why not enjoy objects that make us laugh at what is irreconcilable or purely silly? Anne Lamott captures the effervescence when she defines laughter as "carbonated holiness."

My Texas friend shares my sense of the playful. Inspired by Victorian decoupage screens, she has papered a closet chest with pictures of cats collected through the years. When the chest was nearly covered, she began papering the bottoms of drawers with more fun prints. She even decorates file folders with vintage fashion photographs from old magazines. I treasure one she gave to me, decorated in a vintage print of two friends in hats and gloves strolling through a garden of azaleas and Spanish moss. During a medical odyssey, I received personally-crafted greetings of captivating poems matched with enthralling images from her extensive picture file. Balm to my spirit, their regular appearance in my mailbox heartened recovery.

Antiquing with her is a lark. Amused by the quirky and absurd, we often exclaim together with delight over peculiar discoveries—an armadillo purse, a jeweled horseshoe, a vintage leopard dressing gown. We fuel each other's impertinent sense of style, often prompting the preposterous to follow us home.

My husband's merry mischief keeps the "happily ever after" in our marriage. Even after sleepless nights, he wakes with morning cheer. Michael does not just send flowers . . . he brings me a rose in his teeth. The mantra of an ebullient nature is attitude, attitude, attitude! Cut complaints; seek smiles instead. William James's advice may be just the incentive we need for a positive seismic shift: "To change one's life: Start immediately. Do it flamboyantly. No exceptions."

Sharing a laugh may be the most profound expression of happiness. And learning to laugh at one's self promises inexhaustible amusement. If we can take ourselves less seriously, we will find levity in our own foolishness, and lightness of heart. Reinhold Niebuhr sees a blithe spirit as an unlikely sacrament: "Humor is a prelude to faith and laughter is the beginning of prayer."

Self-Discipline

"Self-command is the main elegance," asserts Ralph Waldo Emerson. A woman who recognizes a clear moral standard, governs her choices, accepts responsibility, and persists toward her goals demonstrates refinement in its truest form.

Standing behind a woman at the customer service counter of a home improvement store, I could not help overhearing her exchange. She was returning a small house plant for a refund. Catching sight of the plant in her hand, I could see that it was not a plant at all, but a dead stick in stone hard soil. It was obvious the plant had not been watered.

The incident indicates a larger societal trend—a quickness to blame and a failure of accountability. Yes, we have the right to choose the expedient and self-serving over the ethical, but how can Americans sustain our lives of enormous privilege if we are unwilling to accept attendant responsibilities? Beyond the obligation inherent in liberty, Pope John Paul II recognizes the prerogative in principles: "Freedom consists not in doing what we like, but in having the right to do what we ought."

Inspiration does not occur by waiting for celestial animation. It demands on regular, rigorous effort. As George Eliot says, "It will never rain roses. When we want to have more roses, we must plant more roses." Developing any kind of excellence—gardening, singing, writing—or committing to self-improvement—exercise, healthy eating—requires not only enthusiasm, but discipline and persistence. Discipline means refining our skills, eliminating what dilutes or derails our efforts. Honing an art or ability may mean less time for other pleasures, but exclusions no longer feel like sacrifices as we begin to achieve our goals. J. G. Holland creates this image of the blessing in work: "God gives every bird his food, but He does not throw it into the nest. He does not unearth the good that the earth contains, but

He puts it in our way, and gives us the means of getting it ourselves." When goals seem distant, discipline fuels our tenacity. St. Francis of Assisi advises, "Start by doing what's necessary, then what's possible, and suddenly you are doing the impossible."

A sharp mind, fit body, and fulfilling relationships all need attention. If we do not fuel them with healthy fare, they will no longer function well. Would we completely neglect any of these dimensions of our lives and still expect our best from them? What about the health of our spiritual lives?

Sunday morning en route to church, I find streets clear and easy to navigate. Worship in a serene setting allows me to focus all my senses on the spiritual. The traffic of the week ahead is what complicates my way. In the jarring, crowded week, I must apply my spirituality. Day by day, I must sort out the extraneous to tend essential matters of the heart, mind, and spirit. Yet the challenge promises enormous gifts, as Helen Keller notes: "When we do the best we can, we never know what miracles await."

Serendipity

Perhaps one of the most unusual outfits I have ever worn was a long, ruddy, shapeless tunic with trailing medieval sleeves, costumed for a program on the life of Joan of Arc, which I was presenting to a classroom of fidgeting elementary students. I was reading a story about Joan as requirement for a college course in children's literature. Just as I was about to dramatize the scene in which she faces accusation of heresy, the fire alarm blared. I dashed down stairs with the kiddies in my floating red gown, looking surely like the fire belle herself. When we returned to the classroom, the prospect of a young girl condemned to a burning death suddenly gained poignancy. Significance comes through personal relevance, which is why we want to seek with our hearts and minds the value in what we often overlook. Samuel Johnson says, "To improve the golden moment of opportunity, and catch the good that is within our reach, is the great art of life."

Busy mothers may wonder how they can possibly savor small moments with all the demands of tending to family, work, and home. If unpredicted detours delay something planned, so what? Postponing has its merits. The most needful demands will surface. Those less critical will fall from the list. The rest are not going anywhere. The pressure to accomplish is often a force we create ourselves. Skip the requirements occasionally, and opt for spontaneity. Children can find adventure and delight in anything. Capture those moments of caprice as they appear, and seize the bliss.

Roman philosopher Seneca knew this truth: "The greatest loss of time is delay and expectation, which depends upon the future. We let go the present, which we have in our power, and look forward to that which depends on change—and so relinquish a certainty for an uncertainty."

I am the world's worst navigator. My husband hates to drive. As newlyweds living in Europe, we discovered the combustible combination. Getting on and off European superhighways could be challenging. An exit may take us unexpectedly through farmyards, past cows, through cobblestone market places while I spun the map in my hands to gain bearing and my new husband admonished me to "Look at the map!" We opened the car's sunroof to release the mounting steam.

On one seemingly simple excursion to France, we left a major roadway to find ourselves in a rural village, following an unanticipated route. The small lane onto which we had turned narrowed and appeared to dead end at the river before us. "Keep going," I instructed, squinting at my road map that showed the road continuing across the river. "This can't be right!" my husband growled in exasperation. We reached the river, where a small sign appeared: "Wait for ferry." Despite our initial apprehension, we had an unexpectedly scenic trip across the river and picked up our route on the other side of our watery detour.

BEING SUSCEPTIBLE TO SERENDIPITY PROVIDES UNIMAGINABLE DELIGHTS. When our mapped route dissolves despite our best planning, a ferry often seems to appear, an alternative means of reaching our next leg of life's road. Being susceptible to serendipity provides unimaginable delights. Even mistakes can be unexpected routes to blessing. Thomas Carlyle maintains that when our eyes are open to awe, "wonder is the basis of worship."

Happiness derives, literally, in the word's origin, from what "hap"pens to us—the surprise, the fortune. The straightest route may be the least interesting. But what surprises may await our meandering and digressions? When we are receptive to novelty, coincidence, the random and improbable, all those little epiphanies

we trip over will prevent us from becoming too predictable and keep us perennially astonished.

My husband Michael shares the credo of Germaine Greer: "The essence of pleasure is spontaneity." He revels in reconnaissance expeditions for novel places and new people. When traveling, we often pursue our separate interests, then rendezvous later to share discoveries. After my sightseeing, he once invited me to meet him at a French bistro he had found, providing explicit directions to the block where it was located, not far from a large plaza. "You can't miss it," he assured me. I walked the indicated block several times, eventually eliminating every establishment it could not possibly be and settling on a doorway with no name nor any indication at all that it led to a public establishment and not to a private residence. Tentatively, I pulled the door, brushed aside a privacy curtain, and stepped over a sleeping dog to find Michael right at home, making friends in his elementary French. He introduced me to the proprietor as though he were an old friend. On another occasion, I met him for lunch after a morning flea-market foray, to find him already on friendly terms with the waitress adjusting his bow tie. Soon he was introducing me to all the staff and an array of guests.

We IMPOSSIBLY CURIOUS CANNOT HELP OURSELVES.

In affordable years before it became a celebrity watering hole, we vacationed on the French island of St. Bart's. Exploring one day, we bumped along rocky roads, through tangled brush, to a bohemian restaurant on the opposite side of the island, far off the beaten path. We were its only customers. After Michael had worked his magic and we were served a sublime tropical lunch on the thatched-roof terrace, the restaurateur retired to his company of friends, inviting us to help ourselves to the kitchen and to spend the afternoon. We indulged in his hospitality, lounging in the hammock of a tamarind tree, where a parrot overhead kept us company. Michael's innate synthesis of curiosity and abandon has nurtured his talent for meeting fascinating folks in out-of the way locales—Tyrolean outlaws, international spies, Russian gypsies, and a paratrooper of the French Foreign Legion. Traveling through life with him is a wondrous excursion. We impossibly curious cannot help ourselves. Dorothy Parker quips, "The cure for boredom is curiosity. There is no cure for curiosity."

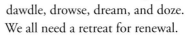

Serenity

In the dizzy, busy blur of modern life, the bedroom can provide a restful haven. Banishing electronics and reserving the room for soothing activity help to eliminate work and stress. Soft tones, comfortable textures, and limited clutter create an inviting space to dawdle, drowse, dream, and doze. We all need a retreat for renewal.

A monochrome palette creates an enticingly soothing effect—a green garden blooming with an array of white flowers, a bath of soft aqueous blues from walls to linens.

An ensemble in a single, soft hue or neutral shade with one stunning piece of jewelry streamlines one's silhouette. Solid, understated colors tend to be easy to wear with hints of brights—a blouse, jacket, or scarf—to highlight skin tone. Busy patterns and florals or too much ornament near the face competes with the subtle shading and sculpting of features. Embellishment often works best in small doses, as in a stunning shawl, smart belt, or great shoes. Extravagance and ostentation are unflattering. Heavily decorated outfits tend to be not only less complimentary, but also more quickly outdated. Tasteful, uncomplicated dressing, on the other hand, creates a no-fail, pulled-together look. After all, style is not about how our clothes look on us, but about how we look in our clothes. A serene appearance can transfer to temperament. "To be beautiful and to be calm, without mental fear," contends Richard Jefferies "is the ideal of nature."

Cooking delicate fish or tender chicken requires a slow, easy simmer at low temperature. Recipes often recommend heating the water only until it "smiles." A gentle tempo, a slowness to boil, and a sensitive touch will make us smile, too. Racing from thrill to thrill is ultimately more exhausting than satisfying. Victor Hugo compares

calm to another languorous delight: "Excitement is not enjoyment: in calmness lies true pleasure. The most precious wines are sipped, not bolted at a swallow."

When it comes to our personal lives, efficiency is often overrated. Who has ever recalled nostalgically the speed at which she turned the pages of her days? What we will remember are the sweet passages— the morning we raked leaves with a grandson and jumped into their piles just to hear them crunch, lunch with our spouse on a secluded terrace that lingered through the afternoon, an evening spent sharing intimacies with a friend. Mary Oliver aspires to "do whatever it is that presses the essence from the hour." Time will keep ticking; we will not. Memories in the making consecrate our book of hours.

A visit to the Dairy Queen was a special outing for our family. I can still recall from childhood the buzz of frenzied moths in a pool of florescent light as we waited at the small screened window for our turn to order, curling fingers around the sticky serving ledge for a better view, always ordering the  same chocolate covered cone with all its sensory delights—soft, hard, sweet, cold—melting already in August heat before we reached the car. Simple moments for a child are often intense and indelible. They are worth remembering . . . and creating.

From the womb we accelerate. Why are motion and speed so compelling? Slaves to our calendars, clocks, and pocketbooks, we are driven to acquire lots that matters little, when what we desperately need is time for repose and reverie. We need moments to meditate and muse, lulls to idle and linger, hushes to play and pray. We need time for combing out life's tangles. Every minute need not be productive. We need a slower cadence, a gentle rhythm. The rests in music are as vital as the notes. They, too, convey the melody. A Thai proverb prompts reflection: "Life is short. We must move very slowly."

Our families need less hurry, too. Husbands need time to decompress, not more items on a "to do" list. Children need room in a week packed with organized activities to explore in unstructured ways, unplugged from electronic gizmos and gadgets. Do children still rustle up games of jacks or jump-rope with friends, play Fox and Geese in a fresh snowfall, or cut out clothes from catalogs to design original outfits for paper dolls? Might they enjoy some traditional pastimes?

Beneath a broad-brim, his weather-sheared face reflected in the airport window. I would have known him anywhere—the prairie-soiled boots, long stretch of jeans, and at his studded belt, the cowboy wore . . . the most current of smart phones. Why did this accessory strike me as so anachronistic? I recognize that executives, professionals, moms, and school children feel compelled to tether themselves to access at any moment, but a cowboy? Why are my sensibilities jarred by the thought that this icon of free spirit and rugged individualism has joined the ranks of the connected? What about life on the range with the horse his only companion? What about silent nights under starry skies? I recognize the stereotype as an idyllic fantasy. I know that today's cowboy is as likely to be contacting an investment broker as a ranch hand, that he may be as interested in headlines as in his herd. Still, I want to think that someone has escaped the electronic lasso. I want to imagine that somewhere personal terrain remains uncluttered by the assault of distant concerns. The cowboy likely counts it progress that his open range extends far beyond the horizon. Still, I have to wonder what our crush of stampeding contacts may trample.

Many of my students today seem increasingly tense. Feet wag, attention drifts, and work is hurried. They are adept at multi-tasking, but their rushing challenges the thoughtfulness that study requires, the steady effort needed to digest information and to acquire skills and knowledge, the critical ability to distinguish what is valid and relevant. They are products of an overextended, yet impoverished culture.

We could all benefit from less pressure, more peace. Calm is required for the deliberation needed to make sound choices and decisions. Certainly we can be both busy and competent, but when stressed, our spiritual grounding may be more susceptible to crowding and compromise.

$\mathcal{C}$ALM IS REQUIRED

FOR THE DELIBERATION

NEEDED TO MAKE SOUND

CHOICES AND DECISIONS.

Television may be among the worst culprits in eroding our serenity. While the medium may include some redeeming offerings, much of its most popular programming—news, talk shows, and dramas—appeal to baser human instincts. Crime, sex, and horror appear commonplace. Assailed by the lurid, salacious, and profane, viewers become inured to depravity. Vapid and fatuous programming debases the intellect. Television's commercial barrage fuels vanity and greed. All these assaults are not innocuous; they are spiritually depleting. Such a powerful societal force is not easy to avoid, but we can cast a more critical eye on what we view, or better yet, turn it off.

How can we avail ourselves of more elevating influences? We might evaluate what we watch, read, and listen to; with whom we associate; how we spend our time. Do any of these displace time better spent in more meaningful, fulfilling ways? Do our contacts and activities promote qualities we want to cultivate? Judicious choices will feed the soul.

According to *The Oxford English Dictionary,* "time" is the most often used noun in our language. It may be also the commodity most often misspent. Why are we rushing into the future, when it will always be there waiting for us? Just now, we need time to "just be."

If we truly desire less aggravation and agitation, why are we not pursuing serenity more assiduously? When our sensibilities are dulled and diffused by the static of noise and motion, how can we find a stillness of spirit? We might begin by committing ourselves to this very moment's object of attention—embracing the blessing in the task at hand, the dear one near. Marya Mannes encourages us to "lie down and listen to the crabgrass grow, / the faucet leak, and learn to love them so." Only when we stop, look, and listen truly can we reach that state of grace which restores a reverence for our God, for our world, and for those around us.

Cannot sleep? Are the same relentless issues wearing a rut in your mind? Try keeping a pad and pen near the bed. Write down those insistent thoughts and concerns. Then adopt Scarlett O'Hara's attitude: Think about them tomorrow. When we shed our worries, Julian of Norwich assures us that "all shall be well, and all shall be well, and all manner of things shall be well."

On the wall of a cousin's home, an heirloom clock kept accurate time for decades, never losing a minute. Its hands passed along the hours as children grew up, married, and parents aged. At the hour of his mother's death, the clock stopped, its hands marking the moment of her soul's departure. The clock had been wound and just minutes before her last breath, had been ticking regularly. As the days following her death resumed routine, the clock was reset. Eventually, the cousin and his wife moved into his parents' home, where the clock remained, continuing its faithful rounds for further decades. Years later, at the hour of his wife's death, the clock again stopped ticking. Both occurrences defy explanation.

Matters of the spirit transcend the limited dimensions of the world we know. Yet, in the hour of loss, when time stands still and silence descends, we recognize that our hours truly are in the hands of our eternal God, and that the love of dear ones lasts beyond the earthly measure of our days.

Shade

Lighting can dramatically affect behavior. I have been in homes with high-wattage, shadeless light glaring above the kitchen table. Having to shout a conversation over a television droning in the background as well, I always feel jumpy in such a setting.

To quiet the mood and turn down the intensity of dinnertime, convert an overhead table light with a dimmer, turn off the television and blaring electronics, play quiet music (let everyone have a turn choosing), and take no phone calls. Family members will soon look forward to the gentler interlude.

Carry the mellow tone throughout the house. Blazing ceiling lights are unforgiving. A shaded chandelier, subtle down-lighting, or torchieres provide more flattering overhead illumination. Select floor, table, or swing-arm lamps near a chair, bed, or divan for reading. To prevent glare and hide hardware, keep lamp shades at eye-level. Ivory, beige, or parchment shades cast warmer light than white ones. All rooms benefit from three-way bulbs and dimmers—dining areas, bathrooms, living rooms, studies, and bedrooms. I love the kindness of lamplight and try to incorporate it in unexpected niches of the house—a warm prelude on an entrance table, a hint of enlightenment tucked in a bookshelf, a placid corner on

Soft, low lighting is one of the easiest and most inexpensive ways of creating a calming atmosphere.

a kitchen counter, a flattering glow in a powder room. Soft, low lighting is one of the easiest and most inexpensive ways of creating a calming atmosphere.

Rooms can be further softened with aging finishes, faded rugs, and such muted hues as dove, cream, and taupe. And nothing cushions the tone of a room more gently or beautifully than the nuances of candlelight or a flickering fire. Outdoor spaces with dappled shade and the liquid silk of moonlight are soothing spots for appetizers or dessert.

We had gone into the garden one evening to watch the long-running dusk ballet of swooping bats feeding on mosquitoes when programming was precluded by an arriving storm. We watched the gathering clouds and dissolving light instead, a lovely production of its own.

One of my favorite sights in all creation is the moon perched in branches of a tree. In the dark tableau, I find God physically in touch with the world. In a crescent moon, I sense our bloated world casting a smudge on the face of God. Basking in a full moon, I feel the return of God's intended glory. And when a great harvest moon beams gold, I hold God's graces close and full. One night we dashed outdoors in our night clothes to catch a rare glimpse of a total lunar eclipse. At its darkest point, the moon's corona still glowed. Despite humanity's dark tendencies, it is reassuring to recognize that we can never fully obscure God's goodness.

Simplicity

To the eye of Leonardo da Vinci, "Simplicity is the ultimate sophistication." A plain background enhances a focal point. On an unadorned black sweater, a sculptural pin stands out. On an expanse of garden green, bright flowers in the foreground grow more vivid. A serene background embosses what matters in bold relief. With diminished distraction, we find it easier to attend to the truly significant.

With basic white dinnerware, we can easily design striking tables. For color, linens are effortlessly adapted to the occasion—formal whites, casual cotton prints, garden florals, and festive brocades. Fabric stores offer inspiration. A length of inexpensive material can be quickly cut and hemmed into colorful napkins and a matching overlay, thrown on the diagonal over a white table cloth. Pretty sheets may double as tablecloths, too.

For a centerpiece, search cupboards, garage, and basement to find fresh ideas for unlikely containers. Try blooming bedding plants from the nursery in a basket; a vase of gold fish; flower heads and floating candles drifting in a shallow crystal bowl; seashells and sand spilling from a beach bucket; or seed packets, garden gloves, and cabbages grouped for seasonal settings. As an alternative to a center arrangement, place small bunches of flowers in tea or julep cups at each setting. Generously strew votives in shimmering glasses about the table. Books make great tabletop props as risers for other focal points or as a statement themselves. They are guaranteed to elicit conversation. Creativity is inexpensive. Spend it lavishly and often for, as John Ruskin notes, "There is no wealth but life."

Why drive distances to a gym to share sweaty equipment, huffing and puffing stale air? To save time, turn on upbeat music or a video to get motivated, stretch, lift hand weights, and exercise in the living

room, then walk
in the fresh air just
outside the door.
Incorporate flexibility,
strength, and aerobics
in a routine you can
maintain. To stay fit,
the only expense is
regular time. What
other investment
offers so much benefit
for so little?

As I watch air passengers cramming belongings into stuffed overhead bins, I hear in my mind the lyrics of a country song, noting there are no luggage racks on hearses. We can drag our excessive baggage through life, but, ultimately, we must leave all accumulations behind. Will we wonder then, why we spent so much of our time acquiring so little of consequence? As Eric Hoffer avers, "You can never get enough of what you don't need to make you happy."

Opening her purse, the woman in line before me handed several bills to the librarian. "Overdue library and video fines are killing me!" she laughed.

Is it amusing that other patrons could not enjoy the books her family held out of circulation; or that her children learned due dates are not really deadlines, that they can pay their way out of broken rules, or that policies for the greater good do not apply to them? When we have much and squander it in even small ways, we can easily grow immune to the effect our behavior has on others. Plato's admonition still serves: "Let parents bequeath to their children not riches, but the spirit of reverence."

Bridal magazines entice brides to mount fairy-tale extravaganzas. Weddings are big business, marketing exorbitant displays at absurd expense. Ironically, while costs of marriages increase, their longevity seems to decrease. Yet often the simplest weddings with intimate receptions are the most lovely and personal. Even Jacqueline Kennedy kept an eye on expenses. She married Aristotle Onassis in an ivory lace dress she had worn a few months previously at the wedding of a friend. Might a young couple better invest in long-term value? Might they give greater attention to knowing each other well and examining compatibility? After all, their commitment is not about the single day, but about all their days ahead together.

Advertising is designed to create craving, but we need not waste our time and resources on buying into this charade. The appeal of glittering acquisition compounds our challenge of distinguishing desire from necessity. Although getting more seduces us, having more tyrannizes us. We become burdened with storing, organizing, and maintaining the congestion of all our paraphernalia.

Nor are the effects of our excess solely personal. Our planet suffers, too. Consider the finite resources destroyed to produce the expendable. Count the toll of all we discard. If we will not restrain our appetites, we may find them controlled for us. A society, a world that consumes beyond its means is not sustainable.

Living a less complicated existence is not such a sacrifice. In fact, selectivity can be liberating. And salutary options are increasing. Living with conscious regard for our planet no longer equates with earth shoes and grass floor mats. Wholesome choices for home, garden, and wardrobe are increasingly chic. Even small changes can make a life of less become a life of so much more. Joseph Hall expresses the value of simplicity: "Moderation is the silken string running through the pearl chain of virtues."

Although we often rail against the finite nature of our time, energy, physical and mental capabilities, we might, instead, be grateful for limitations. These constraints lead us to depend on sources of strength beyond ourselves. We are led to be grateful to God and to others for the graces they bear us. In fact, many of life's delights accompany dreams denied. "If all our wishes were gratified," counsels Richard Whately, "most of our pleasures would be destroyed."

EVEN SMALL CHANGES CAN MAKE A LIFE OF LESS BECOME A LIFE OF SO MUCH MORE.

Simplicity is commonly misunderstood. It does not mean leading a simple-minded unexamined life, but a life which has been carefully regarded in all its complexity to reveal profoundly simple truths. In the humble lies the holy. Friedrich Nietzsche offers this placid aspiration: "Precisely the least, the softest, lightest, a lizard's rustling, a breath, a breeze, a moment's glance—it is little that makes the best happiness."

Space

I grew up in Kansas, a beautiful state with plenty of room. When my sister's mother-in-law arrived from the congested East coast for her son's wedding on the Kansas plains, she traveled through miles of rolling grasslands from the airport. Scanning the unaccustomed open space, she wondered aloud, "What do they DO with all this land?" While stretches of land are used for growing crops and grazing animals, or are set aside for preservation, she was mystified by the lack of industrial, commercial, and residential development.

In wide open regions of our country, breathing room is easy to take for granted. A Chinese gentleman visiting this same Flint Hills area of the state had never experienced a place on the planet without people in sight. He and his wife stood for a long meditative while, mesmerized by the billowing grass, unfettered breeze, swooping birds, and vast vistas to all horizons. Solemnly returning to his host, he remarked on the transcendent experience with great reverence: "This must be what Paradise is like."

I subscribe to designer Emanuel Ungaro's opinion that "true luxury is silence and space." Unfortunately, my fondness for clean lines and elbow room often battle with my nesting instincts, but I aim to reign my twig collecting. Every void need not be filled. Consider how a gallery displays art, with plenty of marginal space. Wall-to-wall stimulation would overwhelm our sensory, emotional, and intellectual response. We better focus on individual works set well apart.

Editing enhances beauty. If we count all our belongings as treasures, we might appreciate them more by putting some items away temporarily, swapping them with others, and enjoying fresh pleasure in them later. As we shed clothes in summer, rolling up carpets creates a cool bare-floor look. Donating books from crowded shelves might free a place for plants. Empty space can inspire possibility and allow

EDITING ENHANCES BEAUTY.

us to savor the splendor of spare. "For it is only framed in space that beauty blooms," Anne Morrow Lindbergh affirms.

Where can we begin to open space? A glance will likely suggest plenty of opportunities—pruning overgrown landscaping, discarding bland recipes, trimming fat, safely disposing of expired medications and old household products, banishing outlived accumulations, reducing trash. Encouraged by results, we may find it difficult to stop. With desktop exposed, files edited, refrigerator cleaned, belongings ordered, we can more readily find what we are looking for—room to breathe and grow. William Morris impels us: "Have nothing in your house that you do not know to be useful, or believe to be beautiful."

The Sublime

A THING OF BEAUTY IS A JOY FOREVER:
ITS LOVELINESS INCREASES; IT WILL NEVER
PASS INTO NOTHINGNESS; BUT STILL WILL KEEP
A BOWER QUIET FOR US, AND A SLEEP
FULL OF SWEET DREAMS, AND HEALTH, AND QUIET BREATHING.
~John Keats

Extraordinary . . . I have never seen anything like it! Extravagant . . . I would never have thought of owning it! Exquisite . . . It takes my breath away!

The sublime and the ridiculous are animating counterpoints. To qualify as sublime, a piece must be truly outstanding, with irresistible allure. The painting, table, or rug must thrill and intoxicate. A distinguished acquisition will punctuate a space with an exclamation point!

French writer Stendhal acknowledges that "beauty is the promise of happiness." On rare occasion, a singular treasure crosses my path and stops my stride. Because it is an indulgence, it is not a splurge I take lightly. I may visit a unique find repeatedly before convincing myself that it is exceptional enough to command the expenditure. At a German flea market, I spied a compelling majolica vase— black and gold vines and leaves embossed on ivory, punctuated by magenta lilies. Beyond my early-marriage budget, I admired its captivating artistry for weeks before succumbing. In our living room, the vase elevates everything surrounding, and makes me smile each time I see it.

A sublime silk dress loses allure if its wearer is tugging or squirming in discomfort. Spectacular shoes need not be excruciating. Fortunately, handsome well-fitting flats and low heels are beginning to become available, for even formal wear. The splendid should not sacrifice comfort, unless it is a fabulous chair for an intimate corner where it will be lightly used as a perch to slip on shoes. While gentle care may be in order for our finest possessions, concern for things too precious dilutes their joy. Whatever delights we claim should be compatible with the way we live and with the welcome we want to extend. Ultimately, as Ralph Waldo Emerson professes, "The ornament of a house are the friends who frequent it."

Texture

Admittedly, my mother's habit of hanging our family's freshly laundered and impeccably ironed clothes in our closets, ready for wearing, left an impression: I do not feel fully dressed unless my clothes are carefully pressed. Not everyone considers ironing a priority, but having clothes pressed to wear eases my morning's rush. I find confidence and comfort in the sheen of polished cotton, the sleekness of silk, the crispness of linen—creases sharp, wrinkle-free. Through the tumble of the day, I will rumple soon enough. At least, I can start the day smartly and smoothly.

In the garden, texture is vital. Mounding peonies, spiky lilies, trailing ivy, glossy gardenia, and prickly juniper are distinguished by shape and feel, variations contributing as much interest as color.

As for dressing, who does not take tactile delight in the heft of tweed, the slip of satin, or the tickle of cashmere?

Texture can be easily overlooked in decorating, but it conveys much of a room's attitude and appeal. Glass, leather, and chrome create sleek

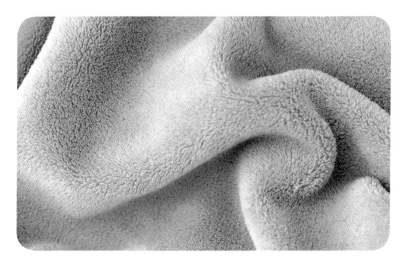

sophistication. Velvet, damask, and fur induce coziness. And anyone will melt in the caress of a voluptuous down-filled comforter.

> AND ANYONE WILL MELT IN THE CARESS OF A VOLUPTUOUS DOWN-FILLED COMFORTER.

Whether in our exteriors or interiors, intention often determines texture. Do we want to invite a handshake, a kiss on the cheek, or a close embrace? Charlotte Moss urges, "Decorate luxuriously, live passionately.'"

When was the last time you were hugged for no other reason than affection? Can you remember when you last felt an arm around your shoulders, your hand clasped, your arm patted, your face stroked? Few of us feel we receive enough human touch. We are hungry for the comfort, communication, concern, and connection conveyed in physical contact. Numerous studies show the remarkable benefits of touch to physical and mental health and well-being. Hugging, touching, and holding hands reduce pain, stress, heart rate, and blood pressure while boosting healing and immunity.

In our American society, increasingly suspicious of unsolicited overtures, we shy from reaching out to others, and yet, we yearn for touch. To satisfy our tactile cravings, we can get a massage, a pedicure, a shampoo. We can cuddle a child or a pet, take up dancing, go for a caressing swim, walk in the breeze, or dig in the soil. If physical touch has never been part of our interaction with family and friends, we can cultivate such intimacy by touching a friend's arm while talking, squeezing a mother's hand, brushing a husband's cheek. Skin is an incomparable conductor of human warmth. In the coarseness of our world today, who can resist the feel of tenderness?

Touch is a particular grace to the elderly. Although skin changes with age, it never loses its sensitivity to palpable pleasures. Let us hold our dear ones close, snuggle them now, and confer sweet blessing. "Love consists in this," explains Rainer Maria Rilke, "that two solitudes protect and touch and greet each other."

Tradition

French soigné applies to a woman who is not just fashionable, but consistently attentive to her appearance, well groomed, and polished. The term connotes a sophisticated elegance, which is never dated or out of style.

When I cull clothes I no longer wear for the thrift shop or church rummage sale, my wardrobe mistakes are usually trendy deviations from the classics. The best fashion choices resist the lure of short-lived trends and opt for what is personally flattering. Lovely patrician styles—straight skirts, classic turtlenecks, well-constructed cardigans, tailored jackets, slim slacks, linen trousers, nude toned shoes, ropes of pearls, silk scarves—can be worn in an infinite variety of combinations and never go out of date. "A classic is a classic," emphasizes Edith Wharton, ". . . because of a certain eternal and irrepressible freshness."

I am often dismayed that fashion cycles seem to rehash the worst of trends, which flattered no one in their first incarnation. Why must we endure endless variations of blouson tops, bell-bottoms, tie-dye, and worn jeans? Why can we not see more elements from the beautiful tailoring of the 1940s instead, incorporated and updated in styles for today?

TRADITION BINDS

US WITH HISTORY,

RESPONSIBILITY,

EXPECTATION.

Tradition binds us with history, responsibility, expectation. It provides continuity and coherence. We discard it at our own peril. Just as customs of

etiquette induce social comfort, formality and convention can ground and guide us. We want to be cautious if embracing the lure of change means discarding established values. Novelty is best judged, with a backward glance, by its long-term human implications. As George Eliot declares, "I desire no future that will break the ties of the past." ✐

Transition

Growing out a hairstyle is difficult. While getting from one cut to another, hair becomes unmanageable, our best styling efforts disappointing. The initial stages of change are challenging. Nothing works as easily or as well as it did . . . or as it will. Struggle is the nature of flux. But if we commit to the process of becoming and focus on the outcome, we can grow to great new lengths. Price Pritchett assures us that "change always comes bearing gifts."

When author Eudora Welty left Mississippi to attend school in the North, her mother sent her beloved camellias by train, an affectionate kiss from her Southern home, assuaging her homesickness and encouraging her to bloom in her distant clime. I have adopted this sweet gesture by carrying floral mementos of

my own home to my Midwestern mother, an avid flower gardener. Because she was committed to my father's care and unable to visit me, the blooms connected our latitudes and longitudes.

Clouds in our lives are not always in the distance, passing over. Sometimes we find ourselves in their midst. Anyone who has flown has experienced the otherworldly view while sailing above a billowing sea of white. As the plane descends through that dense cloud layer, the flight often grows bumpy. Vision is obscured. When we emerge, city lights, fields, and landscapes below return in clear sight. We are

relieved to regain our perspective of distance. Life has these opaque, unsettling periods when clouds engulf us. We cannot see what is above or below, behind or ahead. Some days we do not regain sight until we are nearly touching our craft on the ground again. We recognize these murky spells as part of getting where we are going. Their transitory nature makes us grateful for occasions when we can see a clear horizon approaching from afar, and reminds us to remain buckled until the captain has turned off the seatbelt sign.

Within months of my father's debilitating stroke, my mother and he in his wheelchair were visiting other shut-ins in the nursing home. Despite the life-changing adjustment my father's condition demanded of them, they made no time for brooding over misfortune. Through long experience, they recognize that life's path is seldom straight. They have learned that bends and turns prevent seeing what is ahead and fretting before we reach the next kink in our plans. They have also discovered that a swerve or upset can require a new route or means of transit. They navigate life's passages, adapting to unexpected circumstances with patience and perseverance. I marvel at and am grateful for such parents to emulate. I know their equanimity has much to do with faith and prayer. They rely on God to reveal blessing in plans He has already ordained. From the perspective of Kathleen Norris, "Prayer is not asking for what you think you want, but asking to be changed in ways you can't imagine."

"PRAYER IS NOT ASKING FOR WHAT YOU THINK YOU WANT, BUT ASKING TO BE CHANGED IN WAYS YOU CAN'T IMAGINE."

Vintage

An axiom of Billy Baldwin's legendary decorating is that "nothing is interesting unless it is personal." To me, the most beautiful homes evolve with time. Miscellaneous conglomerations and eclectic layering create an intaglio of personal passions. Embroidered with memories, such interiors resonate with life well-lived.

Cherished keepsakes, suffused with history, can compose magical mélanges. Design a mosaic of ancestral photos or a tableau of family artwork grouped in similar frames. I wish I had kept our well-loved dolls, our childhood books, and the dramatic art of Sunday school leaflets to make heirloom vignettes today. The most valuable collections have neither provenance nor pretension. They are composed of beloved items displayed with nonchalance. Personal relevance instills cachet. Thomas Jefferson states the worth of personal history: "That which we elect to surround ourselves with becomes the museum of our soul and the archive of our experience."

My sister has moved a great aunt's china into her kitchen cabinets. While she seldom retrieved them for use from basement storage, she now enjoys them regularly when entertaining. To keep memories happening, do not be afraid to use vintage favorites.

When traveling, skip the tourist shops and browse local antique stores, art galleries, and artisan boutiques. A hand-carved wooden spoon, for instance, will recall your trip with pleasure every time you use it. My personal penchant is for the eccentric and weirdly wonderful, infused with anecdote.

I like to put old things to new uses. In the kitchen, inexpensive pressed glass bowls serve as cat food and water dishes. A ceramic cookie jar holds tissues. Clove-stuffed pomanders scent the bath in a transferware cachepot. On my desk, a cast iron window box becomes a bookcase; an iron napkin holder offers note paper. In bedrooms, a miniature quilt-work pillow displays brooches. A tapestry becomes a cornice. Filled with potpourri, a crochet purse dangles from a drawer

pull. A lampshade wears a vintage net bolero. A wool rug dresses the divan. Elsewhere, old books serve as risers for lamps and candlesticks.

Antique trays are especially practical—a papier maché tray to collect letters, a silver tray to hold glasses bedside, a porcelain one to organize oils and seasonings near the stove.

One of my favorite uses for a beautiful old frame is hung around a smaller framed art work inside. Wall space between the two frames serves as an additional matting to enhance focus on art.

Antique linens and handwork offer endless decorating possibilities. The faded rose brocade of my grandmother's parlor drapes now covers a pillow. Wide ecru lace embellishes a bronze vanity lampshade. For a feminine tea, floral handkerchiefs from the 1940s and 50s make fun napkins. Beautiful ones trimmed in handmade lace peek over edges of sideboard shelves.

Doilies or remnants cut from less-than-perfect linens can be stitched to contrasting backgrounds for beautiful pillows. Try tablecloths as curtains and table scarves or runners as valances. With imagination, you will find new stories for the rich narratives woven and stitched into heirloom linens.

Another pleasure of seasoned items is wear. Treasure can reside in tarnish and tatters. I like down-at-the-heels glamour and prefer patina to polish. Burnished by time, brass and marble lose their sheen, but achieve more subtle finishes.

If imperfections are bothersome in old linens, conceal blemishes and holes by layering. Fold and roll a small quilt as a bolster to show its best face. And, of course, slip-covers or fresh fabric can give new life to an upholstered piece with fine lines. Aged objects are worth salvaging. They bear timeless appeal in their intrinsic beauty.

Doilies or remnants cut from less-than-perfect linens can be stitched to contrasting backgrounds for beautiful pillows.

"Laces, ivory, silks, and gold, / . . . / Why may not I, as well as these, / Grow lovely growing old?" wonders Karle Wilson Baker. Age is relative. Age is attitude. Most of us would probably say we feel younger . . . most days . . . than our numerical age. Furthermore, the years of age we register do not feel the same as we think they look on someone else. My father seemed completely taken by surprise that he was in his late 90s, and referred to someone in his even later 90s as "that old guy." Milan Kundera contemplates this relative phenomenon: "There is a certain part of all of us that lives outside of time. Perhaps we become aware of our age only at exceptional moments and most of the time we are ageless."

Don't we wish we had known about Sun Protection Factor when we were younger? Though we cannot prevent the sagging with gravity over time, we could have prevented sun damage, wrinkles, brown patches, and age spots. Don't we also wish we had been better about investing, exercising, eating healthy when younger, and, most importantly, nurturing our spirits? Despite regrets, improvement is never too late to begin. Seneca tells us, "Virtue is that perfect good, which is a complement of a happy life: the only immortal thing that belongs to mortality."

Warmth

On a visit to my parents' home, I found my childhood blanket, lumpy from years of use, languishing in a linen closet. Caressing the worn flannel coaxed from memory the tender secret it held. Like many toddlers, I had clung to my baby blanket until it was pilled and threadbare. When our family moved to a new home, I was reluctant to relinquish its comfort. To ease my release, my mother took me to the fabric store, where I chose tiny green leaves on a pale background from an array of beautifully soft flannels. When I returned home from school one afternoon, my mother showed me my fluffy new blanket, perfect for my new big-girl bed. "But where is my old blanket?" I wondered, tears beginning to surface.

"It's right here," my mother comforted me, holding the blanket to a window's light. I used your old blanket as the batting inside this new one." Mother could not have found a more perfect solution. When I rediscovered her treasured gift years later, I knew I wanted to preserve her loving gesture. I carefully took it apart, though the baby batting nearly fell to pieces in the washing machine. Mother, once again, pinned and stitched a new batting inside the thin, faded flannel. I bound it in satin and stitched atop one corner a salvaged piece of the original baby blanket. That blanket which warmed my girlhood remains a cherished memento of my mother's ardent love. My mother demonstrates the spirit Mother Teresa advocates: "In this world we cannot do great things. We can only do small things with great love."

After the inconsolable loss of a feline friend, my husband received a letter in the mail (written in a familiar hand) from his missing pal, assuring my husband of his buddy's safe passage and enduring love. The oft-read note provided a tangible connection to a beloved companion until a time when she could be comfortably released to memory.

William Butler Yeats refers to true love as a "discipline." Some of our sweetest affections are not a matter of treating others as we would like to be treated, but of treating them as they would like to be treated—going out to dinner with a friend whose spirit needs a boost when we would rather spend the evening with a new novel, standing in line for tickets to a sporting event instead of the ballet, or biting teeth marks into our tongue when a teenager begins to interpret concern as nagging. Nothing warms like heartfelt attentions. John Tarrant calls attention "the most basic form of love; through it we bless and are blessed."

NOTHING WARMS LIKE HEARTFELT ATTENTIONS.

Compassion is the gift of encouragement. Compassion is always needed by the fearful, the hurting, and the discouraged among us. Personal charity moves us to observe closely and offer what is most needed—a phone call, food, help with a task, or a ride for a child. Beyond giving, "charity" means cherishing, by recognizing and attending to the needs of others.

When my sister Jolene offered to help following my recent surgery, Michael and I assured her we were managing fine. She showed up anyway, from a distant state, at our front door. The sight of her was so unexpected and welcome that we all dissolved into tears before I had even the presence of mind to invite her in. She helped me bathe and dress, assisted with meals, comforted and supported us both, and tended needs we did not know we had—generous graces of her compassionate spirit.

COMPASSION IS NECESSARY BECAUSE WE CANNOT ALWAYS KNOW THE SECRET SORROWS OF OTHERS.

Compassion may also be the simple gift of listening—not half-hearted hearing while filling the washing machine, but stopping what we are doing, focusing on the speaker, avoiding too many questions, allowing time for sharing thoughts and unraveling concerns. Listening and loving are not compatible with distraction and cannot be hurried.

Compassion is necessary because we cannot always know the secret sorrows of others. Maybe a cranky co-worker's car would not start or she did not sleep well worrying about bills. Perhaps she is tending an ill parent, her child needed a last minute note to the teacher, or the dog threw up on the rug. On top of it all, she may be having a bad hair day. All she needs is a kind word or a little slack. Plato admonishes us, "Be kind, for everyone you meet is fighting a hard battle."

If we do not see eye to eye, consider how we might disagree without being disagreeable. Respect and tenderness are in order. If we listen closely, we may even find greater agreement than imagined. By looking into the eyes of the person speaking, being a patient presence, accepting what the speaker finds important to say to us, we may be compelled to care.

Let us be slower to claim our personal rights and liberties and quicker to demonstrate our respect for one another. Humans were created to reflect God's glory. Are we looking for His splendor in those about us? 1 John 4:10 reads, "No one has ever seen God; but if we love one another, God lives in us and his love is made complete in us."

One of my mother's favorite gifts for brides-to-be, college-bound students, or new apartment dwellers was pillows. Softness is not only her philosophy, but her nature. She is always ready to bolster confidence, soothe feelings, ease a mind, cushion a landing, or cradle a spirit. Her plush gifts may have been challenging to wrap, but I recall my mother's words as she fluffed the bow: "You can never have enough pillows."

No relationship can prosper without respect. Emphasizing the good in each other fosters reciprocity. Let your husband know you are proud of him. Tell him he is a great father, provider, husband, and man. Praise his grilling or plumbing skill or a personal kindness . . . in front of others. Exude extravagant love. Samuel Taylor Coleridge interprets the communion of relationships this way: "The happiness of life is made up of minute fractions—the little, soon-forgotten charities of a kiss, a smile, a kind look, a heartfelt compliment in the disguise of a playful raillery, and the countless other infinitesimals of pleasant thought and feeling."

Avoid criticism. None of us want to be someone else's fixer-upper project. We like ourselves just the way we are, even our unattractive parts, and are not inclined to change. Instead of nagging a daughter about the mess in her room, shower her with compliments on the way she helped a friend. In the grander scheme, will the mess that bothers you really matter, or is it more important that she cultivate the virtue of kindness? Praise is powerful. It can change behavior. We all want to be appreciated. Let us cheer one another on, for "where there is great love," as Willa Cather attests, "there are always miracles."

A student reporter was interviewing me for a profile in the local paper. When he asked of which accomplishment I was most proud, I responded, "My marriage." The young man asked if I were implying that marriage is work, a view conflicting with the romantically exciting way it is often portrayed. I assured him that a marriage does not thrive without a great deal of compromise, concession, and consideration. Love is not just an adjective describing adoration and affection. To be personified, love must become a verb. Marriage is an ongoing labor . . . of love. In the beautiful line of William Blake, "We are put on this earth a little space, / That we might learn to bear the beams of love."

Wisdom

If you could wish for anything, what would it be? Only one wish. Be careful. No, that's a throw-away wish. Try again. If you could wish for ANYTHING, what would it be?

Imagine being faced with this monumental decision. Consider how King Solomon felt when God himself came to him and invited any request. Because Solomon did not seek personal benefit, God granted his desire. He gave Solomon the greatest attribute for which he could have asked, a "discerning" heart. The discernment which God provides is two-fold, intellectual and spiritual. He granted Solomon the wisdom to make well-reasoned decisions and sound moral judgments. God is not a genie in a bottle, but He will grant our prayer for wisdom if we ask Him to help us recognize His will for our lives.

Pope John Paul II writes, "Faith and reason are like two wings on which the human spirit rises to the contemplation of truth; and God has placed in the human heart a desire to know the truth—in a word, to know himself—so that, by knowing and loving God, men and women may also come to the fullness of truth about themselves."

A widely circulated and unexamined fallacy is that everyone is entitled to one's own opinion. Really? Even if it is unreasonable, ill considered, and poorly informed? Unfortunately, powers of intellect are not always given due regard, and, in fact, often seem devalued. "Too often," comments John F. Kennedy, "we . . . enjoy the comfort of opinion without the discomfort of thought." So much in our society is dumbed down, and education itself is too often regarded as a means to an end rather than as a thrilling lifelong pursuit. Sir Isaac Newton expresses the delight in learning: "The more I enlarge the island of knowledge, the more I increase the shoreline of wonder." An agile curiosity is a fulgent treasure, worth burnishing.

Information is not knowledge. Information is the raw material of study, experience, and instruction. Knowledge is derived from that material by applying intellect. We learn by gaining awareness and understanding of what we encounter. Proverbs 24:3-4 provides this memorable metaphor: "By wisdom a house is built, and through understanding it is established; through knowledge its rooms are filled with rare and beautiful treasures."

Today technology allows faster access to more information, when what we need is slower perusal of vital and complicated matters in greater depth. We have access to the world, but we do not always know what to make of it. Too much information can make us feel confused, overloaded, and incompetent. The sheer volume of information can be intimidating.

Whether considering an appropriate mattress, vitamin supplement, medical treatment, investment, political candidate, or viewpoint, we can become anxious when faced with so many criteria to examine, so many possibilities and perspectives. In our frustration, we may give up trying to figure out the well-reasoned choice, solution, or answer and settle for the easiest or most immediately satisfying. We may leave "experts," perhaps no more capable than we, to sort out complexities and provide us with their version of significance and truth. But if we are disinterested in their means of judging and dispense with making the effort to understand, we relinquish control and abdicate responsibility.

Some decisions do not call for intense scrutiny. In less consequential cases, we may want to settle for adequate rather than best. For other decisions that require exploring ramifications in considerable depth, uncertainty and hesitation can be positive. As we weigh critical issues, plenty of questions are in order. Developing our powers of discernment will help us to determine which matters deserve attention and to make reliable choices. "There are no easy answers," observes Ronald Reagan, "but there are simple answers."

Language is our principal means of clarifying and articulating thought. As images increasingly replace words in our culture, the arts of critical thinking, disciplined study, and ethical deliberation are withering. When a society becomes unaccustomed to critically examining what is heard and read, those skills atrophy. As lines between entertainment, fact, and fiction become blurred, the ability to determine validity and significance erodes. We sorely need to cultivate those faculties required for making perceptive and rational judgments.

How do we make the right choice from myriad options, decide when to heed or discount conflicting advice, or sort out the salient and significant in complex issues? How do we know what

WHEN CONSIDERING

MORAL AND ETHICAL

QUANDARIES, WE NEED

ABSOLUTES, NOT AMBIGUITIES.

standards to apply? And as we challenge assumptions, how do we avoid relinquishing our principles? When considering moral and ethical quandaries, we need absolutes, not ambiguities. In an often unreasonable and irrational world, we can find definitive answers only in the spiritual realm. The sole reliable source of guidance is God. Romans 12:2 counsels, "Do not conform any longer to the pattern of this world, but be transformed by the renewing of our mind. Then you will be able to test and approve what God's will is—his good, pleasing, and perfect will."

Desirable spiritual qualities may seem conflicting. We are advised to be bold yet restrained, disciplined yet flexible, confident yet humble, assertive yet patient, private yet involved, conservative yet generous. We wonder whether harmony is always desirable and at what expense? Wisdom embraces paradox and reconciles apparent contradiction. Proverbs 8:11 tells us that "wisdom is more precious than rubies, and nothing you can desire can compare with her."

Although we will never achieve our best intentions in a lifetime, we can aspire to be wise and virtuous. With whispers and subtle assurances, God comes to us as we cultivate dignity and reverence. We are always His work in progress. In designing our lives, the wisest decision we may make is asking God to make us noble, pure, and lovely.